Explore the Power of
ASTROLOGY

Dr A.P. Parashar
Dr Vinod Kumar Parashar

UNICORN BOOKS Pvt. Ltd.

Distributors
PUSTAK MAHAL

Publishers
UNICORN BOOKS, New Delhi-110002

E-mail: unicornbooks@vsnl.com
Website: www.unicornbooks.in • www.kidscorner.in

Distributors
Pustak Mahal, Delhi
J-3/16, Daryaganj, New Delhi-110002
☎ 23276539, 23272783, 23272784 • *Fax:* 011-23260518
E-mail: info@pustakmahal.com • *Website:* www.pustakmahal.com

Sales Centre
10-B, Netaji Subhash Marg, Daryaganj, New Delhi-110002
☎ 23268292, 23268293, 23279900 • *Fax:* 011-23280567
E-mail: rapidexdelhi@indiatimes.com

Branch Offices
Bangalore: ☎ 22234025
E-mail: pmblr@sancharnet.in • pustak@sancharnet.in
Mumbai: ☎ 22010941
E-mail: rapidex@bom5.vsnl.net.in
Patna: ☎ 3294193 • *Telefax:* 0612-2302719
E-mail: rapidexptn@rediffmail.com
Hyderabad: *Telefax:* 040-24737290
E-mail: pustakmahalhyd@yahoo.co.in

© Copyright : Author

Cover Design : UNICORN Graphics

ISBN 81-780-6064-7

Edition : December 2006

Printed at : Unique Colour Carton, Mayapuri, Delhi-110064

Dedicated to the late

Pt. K D Shastri (Dholpur)
&
Pt. Laxminarayan Sharma (Ajmer)

Preface

Most people who have a little or no knowledge of astrology don't believe in its validity and truthfulness. They disown it on the pretext that astrology is a hoax and has nothing to do with human behaviour, conduct, luck or future.

Like some of these people, I too dismissed any thoughts that could carry me into the vicinity of astrology when I was 20 years old. Such thoughts pervaded me until I turned 25 when, after graduating in English literature from Agra University, I applied for a senior position in the Police Department. As I was physically very fit and comparatively alert mentally, I was confident of being selected. When I had been selected and was about to proceed for six months' training prior to final absorption in the department, my widowed mother persuaded me to consult a renowned astrologer. She believed the astrologer could tell me whether the line of action I intended to pursue was correct or not. Initially, I declined to follow her advice, but as she was apprehensive about my joining the police force and pestered me to consult the astrologer, I agreed to see him.

Before I met the astrologer, it so happened that I had received a letter of appointment as a teacher from the State Department of Education. In fact, that letter helped my mother put more pressure on me to change my mind and take up a teaching job. As her insistence on my meeting the astrologer gradually increased, I yielded to her pressure.

The revered old man sitting on a mat spread on the floor welcomed both of us and inquired what had brought us there. After a preliminary talk on how things were, my mother asked him a direct question: 'Out of the two jobs, which one should my son join to be successful in life?' She then gave him my horoscope. Opening the pages of the horoscope the old man made some caiculations. A while later, he told my mother, 'Your son will have better luck in teaching.' After a pause, he said that though the stars were quite favourable even if I joined the police force, it would be better if I chose teaching. This helped my mother persuade me to stay with teaching. She advised me to stick to what the astrologer had predicted.

Later, we left the old man's house. On the way home, I told my mother that I did not agree with the astrologer's predictions and would surely join the police force, as this was my dream for a couple of years.

A couple of days later, it was time for my departure to the city where I had to join duty prior to proceeding to the police training school. Contrary to my mother's desire, I left home and reached my destination.

Two days later, after the preliminary rituals were completed, my mind suddenly started thinking about the astrologer's predictions. Thirteen men, including myself, had been selected and given railway tickets to proceed to Bihar to join the training school. Along with the others, I had reached the railway station on time but with a double mind. There was still time to join the teaching job. The more I tried to dispel the astrologer's prediction, the more disturbed I felt.

As the time approached to board the train that had already steamed into the platform, I hurriedly wrote a short note to the concerned officer telling him I was unable to proceed to the training school. Handing over the letter to one of my colleagues, I boarded another train to report for the teaching job.

In a doleful mood but under the influence of an unusually strong inner voice, I joined the teaching profession. In fact, I had hardly dreamt of becoming a teacher. But as luck would have it, I started my life's journey as a teacher without any interest in the job. Sometimes, I cursed the astrologer for his prediction. Perhaps his prediction had exerted a psychological effect on me and impelled me to become a teacher.

'Was I really destined to lead life this way?' This was the question that often pervaded my moods making me restless for hours. It was really painful to think about it. Though my mother was extremely happy about my decision, I was burning with agony and dismay. I developed a great dislike towards astrology for obvious reasons.

During those depressing moments, a thought suddenly leaped into my mind. 'Why not study astrology and ascertain whether the astrologer who had doomed my future was right or not?' It was almost 45 years ago when such a thought leaped into my mind. I started from scratch.

Since then I have learnt a lot. Whatever I have learnt is very interesting and inspiring. But I feel that I know very little about this heavenly subject, although I have studied hundreds of horoscopes so far. Everyday dozens of people consult me mainly on issues relating to the marriage of children, finances, luck, the future life they need to pursue etc., but to my great amazement I have never seen two identical horoscopes. Many return if they are satisfied. But if I have ever failed, I've always re-examined the cause of my failure.

My long experience in this field has led me to believe that astrology is more than a science. If ever I failed to predict correctly, it is because of my inability to peep into the hidden layers of this vast ancient knowledge. At this point around 25 years ago, my second son, Dr V.K. Parashar, started showing great interest in astrology. He would often discuss matters relating to the subject. It led to new visions in the field and gradually enriched both of us in various ways. In view of all those perceptions that resulted as a consequence of gathering new knowledge on the basis of the analysis of new charts (*kundalis*), I venture to reveal certain strong beliefs and implore you to learn astrology without a biased mind. Although the content is self-explanatory, the following lines contain a brief preview.

The first chapter starts with the Zodiac Sun signs and dates, both mainly from the Indian point of view. The second chapter contains the basics of astrology and the meaning of the rising sign in the ascendant (first house) of a chart. Besides, defining the characteristics attributed to a rising sign and the 12 Zodiac houses, it also contains details on how to make one's own chart.

The third chapter deals with the transits of the planets through the 12 Zodiac signs and the houses, and their most strong and weak positions. Finally, the findings have been concluded in the fourth chapter by expounding the meaning and strength bestowed by the planets' aspects on the houses. It also explains how the ownership of the planets and their debilitated and exalted positions influence people. The meaning and strength of various *yogas* found in the charts, including the analysis of a dozen case studies of certain people whose charts consist of some important combinations (*yogas*) have been explained. The charts (*kundalis*) presented in the fourth chapter are real and astrologically true. Of their own accord, most persons supplied the charts analysed in the last chapter. A good number of reference books were used to enrich the material. These books are indicated in the Reference section at the end of the fourth chapter.

Before concluding, I would like to thank my eldest son, Suresh Parashar, whose deep knowledge in the subject helped us make relevant changes wherever necessary. I would also like to thank my youngest son, Sanjaya Parashar, and my daughter, Vinita Sharma, who extended abundant facilities to complete this work.

3rd March 2004   **—Dr A P Parashar**
Email: *ap_98607@yahoo.co.in*

Contents

○❖○

Chapter One

Impact of Sun Signs

Zodiac Signs

Both the Sun and the Moon influence human beings in terms of their physique, personality, health, complexion, wealth, vocation, emotional state, love, success and failure, etc. The physical characteristics of men and women, the amount of energy and the agility they possess are primarily influenced by their Sun signs (*rashis*). The Moon signs govern humans' emotional behaviour, feelings and love activities. But the Moon stays in a sign for only about two and a half days. The Sun stays in a sign for almost one month; therefore, its impact is more on humans. Consequently, people bear most of the characteristics displayed by that sign. As the Moon transits from one sign into another, it primarily affects humans' moods and feelings only.

Astrologers generally take into account the Sun signs to predict human characteristics, nature and other qualities. In view of this, we present the Zodiac Sun signs and dates from the Indian point of view. The Western astrological calendar differs from the Indian calendar, as according to Western astrologers the Sun transits from one sign into another around the 21st day of a month. For example, Western astrologers reckon that the Sun transits in Aries around 21st March and stays in that sign until 20th April. But from the Indian point of view it enters Aries on 14th April and stays there until 13th May. *However, the celebrities indicated under each sign have been chosen from both the Western and Indian point of view, irrespective of variation of dates.* The following table is based exclusively on the Indian calendar. But the characteristics of an individual born in Aries, either according to the Western or Indian astrological system, should not vary much.

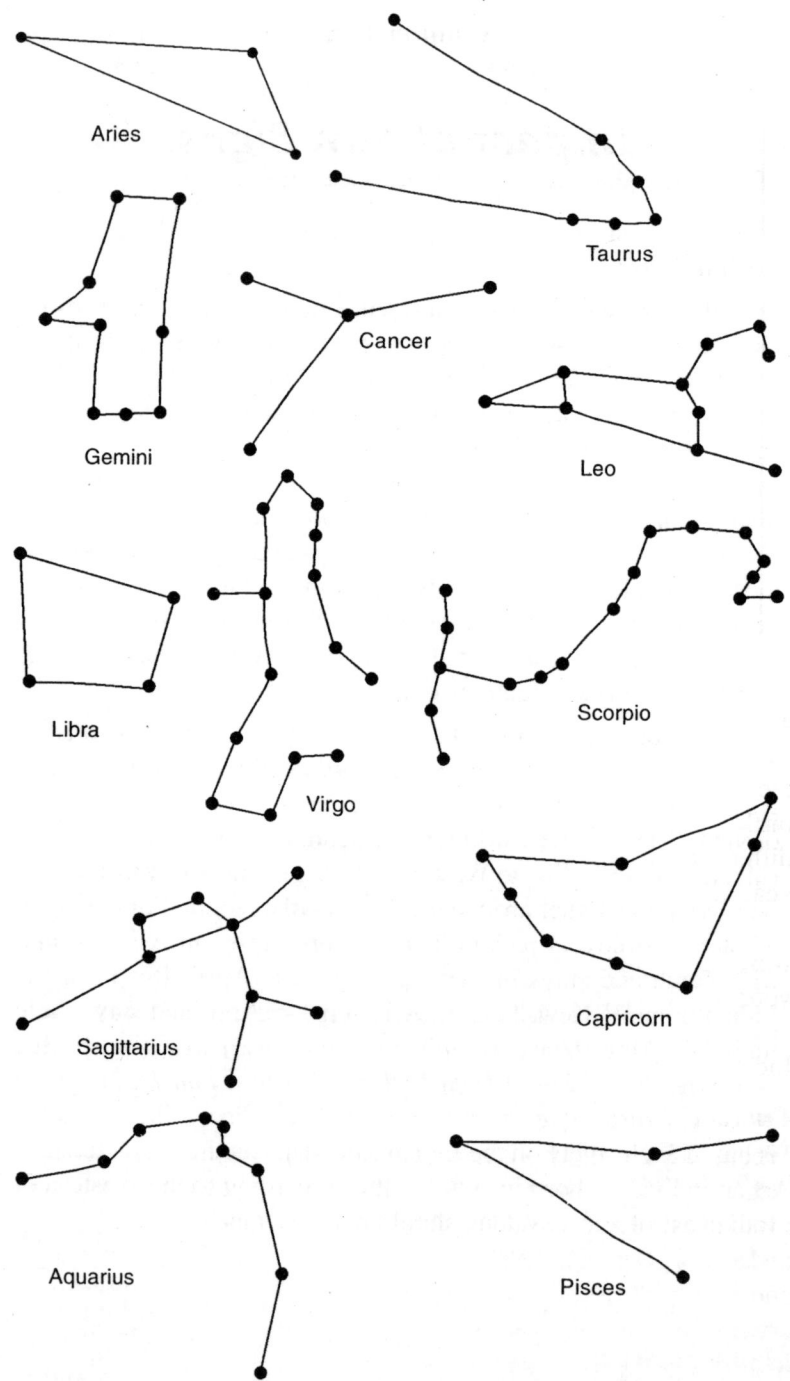

Aries

Taurus

Cancer

Gemini

Leo

Libra

Virgo

Scorpio

Sagittarius

Capricorn

Aquarius

Pisces

Table A

Sun Signs Corresponding to the Indian Calendar

Signs	Dates
Aries	April 14 to May 13
Taurus	May 14 to June 13
Gemini	June 14 to July 13
Cancer	July 14 to Aug. 13
Leo	Aug. 14 to Sept. 14
Virgo	Sept. 15 to Oct. 14
Libra	Oct. 15 to Nov. 13
Scorpio	Nov. 14 to Dec. 13
Sagittarius	Dec. 14 to Jan. 13
Capricorn	Jan. 14 to Feb. 13
Aquarius	Feb. 14 to March 13
Pisces	March 14 to April 13

If you are born on the first or the last day of a Sun sign, astrologically, you are born on a cusp (*sandhi kal*). If that is the case, you will perhaps benefit from reading your own Sun sign and the Sun sign that ends or begins right before or after your date of birth. But on account of leap years and other factors, time zones differ. When the Sun changes from one sign to the other in a leap year, the signs vary from year to year. So, if you are born quite close to changing dates (or the cusp) and wish to find out exactly which sign you were born under, you will probably need to have your own personal horoscope drawn up. Therefore, the above dates are guidelines primarily. We would advise you to consult the Indian calendar (*panchang*) to be more accurate in that respect.

Characteristics

When the Sun enters the Zodiac sign of Aries it is almost springtime. According to traditional astrology, Aries is hot, dry, cardinal, masculine and ruled by Mars. The Sun is exalted (strong) in Aries and Saturn is debilitated. The sign is connected with new beginnings and powerful initiatives and may tend towards violence, cruelty and crime. An individual born in this Sun sign may be extremely God loving and highly religious.

Aries

Dates: Hindu Calendar April 14 to May 13	
Element:	Fire
Ruling planet:	Mars
Symbol:	The Ram
Colours:	Red, scarlet, carmine
Gem:	Amethyst, *manak*
Best friends:	Sagittarius and Leo
Virtues:	Loyalty and daring
Weaknesses:	Impatience, overreactions, dreamy
Celebrities:	Sachin Tendulkar, Pt Ravi Shankar, Rabindranath Tagore, Marlon Brando, Eddie Murphy, Gregory Peck

An Aries person tends to think quickly. His mental as well as physical wheels move very rapidly. He is not afraid to give opinions or share statements. Even if the Aries person knows that his viewpoint is not quite popular or welcoming, he will not hesitate to speak his mind. It is obvious that Aries does not have much patience. As Aries is the first sign of the Zodiac, he has the initial spark of cosmic expression within. That provides him great enthusiasm, energy and curiosity. Many inventive and pioneering minds have been born in the Aries sign, including some great astrologers of the world. Aries possesses fire (energy) inside, loves to lead and feels happiest when he is free and independent. He does not accept any kind of restrictions.

In general, Aries is dedicated and enthusiastic, but can become very negative when his health is poor or is influenced by negative thoughts. Then, like a punctured balloon, he is deflated. On such occasions, when he is surrounded by doleful (sad) moods, he sinks into his own self. Therefore, an Aries person should always try to look ahead to the future. But it is also true that bad days don't keep an Aries man down. He is a natural fighter. Aries not only possesses psychological and emotional strength, he also has physical power. Astrologically it is easy to reckon why Aries is such a great warrior. Mars, the ancient god of war and aggression, governs the

14

Aries sign. It is possible that an Aries person can marry in haste. He can even buy property without having worked out how to pay off the loans incurred, if any. Even if he feels bad about some things that have occurred in his life, he has it in him to turn them into blessings in disguise.

Being a fearless person, Aries is often a born adventurer. Such a person will always enjoy reaching the top. This is the reason that so many of them make it as heroes, movie stars, private detectives, sports stars, fighter pilots, great writers, entertainers and military generals. A good thing about Aries is that he does what he says. And he means what he says. He is quickly bored with routine and repetition. Such a person loves variety. There is no finish line for Aries. He does not stop when others would like to The aforesaid characteristics are presented in a table below, indicating benefits and shortcomings of Aries in general.

Table 1
Benefits and Shortcomings of Aries

Characteristics	Advantages	Shortcomings
Aggressive	Gets what he really wants	Tends to live dangerously
Adventurous	Gets the most out of things	Tries many things at a time
Bright	Thinks instantly	Shows off at times
Highly competitive	Loves to win	Plays dirty at times
Confident	Likes to take chances	Doesn't prepare himself
Dramatic	Attracts attention	Creates fuss about nothing
Energetic	Possesses great stamina	Spent out without reason
Enthusiastic	Holds great hope	Desires to go too far
Dauntless	Faces adversity happily	Likely to get into accidents
Impulsive	Exciting	Often incurs trouble
Restless/impatient	Desires to do a lot	Short-tempered
Optimistic	Looks at the bright side	Has low spirits when sad

Characteristics	Advantages	Shortcomings
Progressive	Open-minded	Often restless
Selfish	Does what he wants	Not very reasonable
Unrestrained speech	Straightforward	Can be offensive
Full of energy	Abundant strength	Explosive at times

Although Aries women display some of the above traits, we define their characteristics separately, as they possess something different from men.

An Aries woman is an idealist and values truth and justice. She is ardently loyal. If she loves someone, she is prepared to die for him if necessary, such is her devotion for her man and family. She is warm-hearted, generous, demanding and unpredictable. As she is naturally independent, she likes to lead a life of her own. Hardly ever timid, she is quickwitted, assertive and outspoken, as the masculine planet of war, Mars, governs her. Thus, she has great physical strength and power of endurance.

Whether walking, driving or making love, an Aries woman usually leads the field. She may have big feet or big hands or unusual features, but she is still very attractive. She is often overwhelming. She cannot tolerate her own weaknesses. Often she is not afraid of living life to its fullest. It gives her great courage. She has her own strong beliefs and possesses complete confidence in miracles. As she is an adventurer, she likes to take risks. She is selfish at times. She is often well informed. She wants to help the weak and the needy people.

An Aries woman is not keen on marriage and may also be less interested in playing the role of a mother. She prefers to retain her independence. We know an Aries woman who, after becoming a widow, never desired to remarry. She had a daughter to take care of. If someone tried to woo her, she refused to be tied down, although she was hardly 30 years old then.

But an Aries woman may be drawn to a man who is very strong, powerful and sensitive. She will like a man who lets her be her own person. She thrives in careers that offer lots of variety, spontaneity and physical expression. She can be a great dramatist, a businessperson, a sportswoman and a successful executive.

Taurus

Dates: Hindu Calendar May 14 to June 13	
Element:	Earth
Ruling planet:	Venus
Symbol:	The Bull
Quality:	Stability
Colours:	Orange, earth tones
Gems:	Diamond
Best friends:	Virgo, Capricorn
Weaknesses:	Stubborn temperament, lacking flexibility
Celebrities:	Sigmund Freud, Florence Nightingale, Katherine Hepburn, Queen Elizabeth

Characteristics

The Zodiac symbol, the Bull, displays very prominently Taurus' character on the people in many ways. It represents strength, persistence, stubbornness and determination. As the ruling planet is Venus, the goddess of beauty, it represents the arts, pleasure and emotions. It signifies honour, intelligence, eloquence, loyalty, integrity, popularity and courage.

As Venus is a celestial entity, it often makes one a good-looking person. Venus will not let him/her miss out on inheriting some of her great physical gifts. Since Venus rules Taurus, persons born under the sign love treasures and pleasures. Lots of Taurus-born people are extremely successful and wealthy, either through their own talents, through association with the right people or through marriage. Because Venus is the planet governing the Sun sign, one often possesses great creativity that can express itself on many different levels. It may show up in writing, music, gardening, painting, and involvement in fashion, etc. As Taurus is an earth sign, one who is born under this sign may have a practical sense for survival, which can get him through life's challenges and roadblocks. Most Taurus people are well organised. They take care of everything they possess and love to live in the most comely surroundings. Their weaknesses are self-discipline, stubbornness and depression. Some of the above characteristics of Taurus are listed in tabular form below. It also contains their drawbacks and merits, which the Sun sign in Taurus often endows them with.

Table 2

Benefits and Shortcomings of Taurus

Characteristics	Advantages	Shortcomings
Artistic	Inborn talent	Eccentric taste
Abundantly affectionate	Warm-hearted	Can smother friends
Calm	Stable in crises	Slow mover
Creative	Self-expression	Strives to reach the top
Firm	Reaches final goals	Single-track outlook
Friendly	Appreciative of others	Shows off
Kind-hearted	Well liked	Easygoing
Loyal	Trustworthy	Critical of others
Self-indulgent	Self-rewarding	Fault finding
Possessive	Caring	Controlling
Quiet	Possessing inner strength	Restraining emotions
Thoughtfully respectful	Exhibiting gratitude	Dislikes appreciating
Sensual	Pleasure seeking	Difficult to satisfy
Systematic	Highly organised	Obsessed

A Taurus woman has great qualities like patience, understanding and thoughtfulness. She can also be stubborn but is exceptionally kind-hearted and takes care of the people around her. She adopts orphans and works for charitable causes. She can act as a great citizen of the world. She is special as she cares about other people. She is honest, sincere and usually humble. She is quite clever at saying what she wants to say, without being direct. She can hide her deepest thoughts if she likes. Her home is often a reflection of Venus, but she can also be the worst-dressed woman at times. She loves to travel, but in her everyday life she likes a regular routine. Thus, she resists change. Therefore, a Taurus woman is at times complex, social and friendly as well. She has amazing self-control. She adores animals. Some Taurus women are anti-social – keeping distance from the world at large, preferring their own company. But generally, most Taurus women are warm, affectionate and sensitive.

When a Taurus woman is cold on romance, she often becomes distant and independent. As the planet Venus governs her, art and pleasure rule a Taurus woman. She likes visiting museums. She is often looking for a strong and manly type of male, who works hard, plays hard and does not mind her shopping habits. She has an inborn desire for finery, luxury and praise. Anyone who treats her like a goddess is treated like a god himself. As a mother, a Taurus woman can be most devoted, attentive, patient and preserving.

A Taurus woman has a wide range of different careers. She can make quite a sensitive teacher or instructor. She can work in the areas of security and finance. She will be most suited in companies that deal with the arts, hairstyle, make-up and fashion. She can also work as a tourist guide. She is generally good in client services and public relations, but at times may face difficulties as a saleswoman. Many Taurus women are music lovers and are gifted with some form of creativity.

Gemini

Dates: Hindu Calendar June 14 to July 13	
Element:	Air
Ruling planet:	Mercury
Symbol:	The Twins
Quality:	Flexibility
Colours:	Blue, white
Gems:	Aquamarine, *panna*
Best companions:	Libra and Aquarius
Virtues:	Creativity, shares dreams with others
Weaknesses:	Self-doubts, unfounded fears, inconsistent moods
Celebrities:	Prince Philip, Prince William, Bob Dylan, Salman Rushdie, Clint Eastwood, Marilyn Monroe

Characteristics

A Gemini uses tremendous amount of energy in thinking. His mind seldom stops working even when asleep. Many Gemini men have made a profession as actors, entertainers, and role players. Although a Gemini person is often most charming and accommodating, he can be unbelievably contradictory when it suits him. He has great ideas, moments of great insight, and great ability to inspire others with his thoughts. Because Mercury is the ruling planet, he can also be one of the greatest thinkers and businessmen. His thoughts are far more potent than he possibly realises. One of his shortcomings is not keeping anything secret and taking great delight in disclosing what he knows. If he can keep secrets, he may prosper all the more. Gemini is often friendly, curious, passionate, ambitious and resourceful too. Since his symbol, the Twins, represents his ability to see and appreciate at least two sides of every issue, it makes him diplomatic at times.

He loves travelling. He has abundant mental and physical energy – a gift from planet Mercury. He has plenty of enthusiasm too. He can change mental gears in no time but on account of his extreme curiosity, he is sometimes misunderstood. He has great capacity to imbibe loads of information. Since he is often mentally overactive, he is seldom happy at heart. He has curiosity about life. His desire to learn all sorts of things triggers enthusiasm. He uses his insights in many ways, which could lead-to either artistic or creative directions. As he is interested in many different things, it can be hard for him to focus on just one or two at a time. Consequently, he can get easily sidetracked, heading into the opposite direction.

One of his greatest strengths is the ability to think very quickly and adapt easily to new circumstances. He is, therefore, highly resourceful and able to transform a disaster into something good. But his quick wit can be stinging. When emotionally injured, he can hurt a lot. Most Gemini persons love to be left alone with their thoughts and books. They are versatile and difficult to pin down. But most of them are wonderfully flexible and curious to learn everything. Such people have great desire to communicate and are open change. Let us observe the above qualities in tabular form.

Table 3

Benefits and Shortcomings of Gemini

Characteristics	Advantages	Shortcomings
Ambitious	Self-starter	Takes plenty of liabilities
Adaptable	Unbound, free	Loses interest often
Charming	Can be spellbinding	Misleading
Clever	Thinks instantly	Indecisive
Expressive	Lucid communicator	Exaggerator
Friendly	Can influence promptly	Can be defenceless
Intelligent	Can apply ideas	Unusually critical
Inventive	Insightful	Indulges in great lies
Passionate	Enthusiastic	Single-track mind
Restless to learn	Productive	Complaining unrealistically
Romantic	Lives in fantasies	Too imaginative
Sentimental	Welcomes others	Often depressed
Multi-talented	Can visualise different options	Indulges in many activities

   A Gemini woman can do two things at a time. She does not like to wait for others but likes others to wait for her. She loves drama, change and adventure. She seeks variety in all areas of her life and hates repetition and routine to a large extent. Quite often she chooses a wrong partner and has frequent problems with him. The Gemini woman can make a great friend but a tough foe too. She can bring colour and great resources on many different levels into other people's lives. She is seldom short of words, loves to exchange ideas and can discuss every aspect of an issue with anyone. It is difficult to pin her down. She can be mischievous and sometimes fickle too. A Gemini woman can indulge in gossip and waste time in shopping. She is usually interested in solving her own problems and of others too. The Gemini woman is usually quite compassionate and has many hobbies. She is very stable in love and happy with her family. She often displays a brilliant sense of humour. She can be totally possessive. She can make a great mother and play a good role as a single parent.

She is best in the careers of sales or promotions, public relations and advertising. She can also be quite a successful author, a good actress, serve as a good secretary, hostess, teacher and professional speaker.

Cancer

Dates: Hindu Calendar July 14 to Aug. 13	
Element:	Water
Ruling planet:	Moon
Symbol:	The Crab
Quality:	Cardinal (activity)
Colours:	Silvery grey
Gem:	Pearl, moonstone
Best friends:	Pisces and Scorpio
Virtues:	Inner (soul) power, intuition
Weaknesses:	Cynical attitude, negative thinking, depressive disposition
Celebrities:	Dalai Lama, Harrison Ford, Tom Cruise, Sir Edmund Hillary, Nancy Reagan, Nelson Mandela, Ernest Hemingway

Characteristics

Those born with the sign Cancer are hard on the surface but soft from inside. At times a Cancer person may take a hard line, almost aggressive. But such aggression is often due to self-defence. He makes an excellent parent. He is sentimental and possesses good memory. He is always protective towards younger members of the family. He is quite moody and sensual in love. A Cancer person is likely to make a good friend, though he may be very choosy in this respect. But once he has made his choice, his friendship will remain firm and deep. A Cancer person can be nice at times and may not be as nice at other times. He is often just like the moon. When full, it is brilliant but at its lowest ebb, it is dull. His emotional state is affected by anything, whether big or small, by the weather or even by a movie.

However, a Cancer person's path in life may not be easy because many factors influence him at every moment. As his ruling planet is the Moon, his emotional world is in constant flux. Cancerians who can learn to balance their emotions and rely upon their instincts and intuitions to guide their decisions, do better in life. A Cancer person may often dwell in extremes because, like the Moon, he is naturally an extremist. Experiencing many ups and down, a Cancer person can sometimes be a true test of patience for others. He can also be very difficult to know because of his sudden changes in mood, like his Zodiac sign.

He has such a great wealth of ideas to call upon that he is generally highly creative. With a usually confident appearance, he tries to project that he is constantly right. However, the truth is that he is not. But he is mostly quite independent and does not like to seek others' advice or help. Because of the extreme nature of the sign in which he is born, he spends a lot of time feeling totally happy or completely sad. Thus, a Cancer person often lives within the emotional world that rules him from within. Making careful decisions can be his biggest challenge, as his head and heart are constantly in conflict with each other. This is the reason why a Cancer person born at the time of the full moon is quite different from one who is born on a new moon, or the phases in between. But if he is born during a more favourable moon phase, his feelings are often more balanced and he experiences less disturbances and emotional turmoil. Thus, consistency is one of his major problems.

If he desires to live happily, he needs to build better confidence in life. His psychic senses, together with his emotions, make him very powerful. If he can combine these, he may be able to negotiate matters better and turn them in his favour. It is very likely that a Cancer person is keen to marry and desires to settle down with a permanent partner in life. His greatest strength is his deep understanding of human nature. Sometimes he can know in advance what other people think. He is highly sensitive and hardly forgives and forgets any wrong done to him. He is often a reliable friend, although slow to build up intimacy and trust. For the reference of the reader, the above characteristics are presented in tabular form.

Table 4

Benefits and Shortcomings of Cancer

Characteristics	Advantages	Shortcomings
Confident	Self-esteemed disposition	Awe inspiring
Creative	Uncommon expression	Many ideas at a time
Charming	Liked by others	Manoeuvring
Emotional	Lofty feelings	Ups and downs in moods
Imaginative	Creative viewpoint	Overreacts
Intuitive	Active conscience	Highly irrational at times
Moody	Not predictable	Difficult to deal with
Patient	Hard working	Dull and doleful
Protective	Fights with inner strength	Hates failing
Receptive	Open to new thoughts	Confused by many views
Sensitive	Full of emotions	Doleful and sad
Sympathetic	Tender hearted	Involved in others' problems

A **Cancer woman** wears one of the most feminine signs of the world. It is her most unique power. Therefore, she can also be complex, stubborn and manipulative. She also knows how to make others feel loved and appreciated. She loves modesty and is also tough. At the same time, she is considered to be a great seductress. She can make men surrender their wealth and heart to her. When she fails in love, her ego goes wild. In fact, love and sex often don't go together for a Cancer woman. Like her moods, she is at times complicated and can be attracted physically to someone with whom she is not in love. But she can fall in love with someone else, with whom she does not want to make love all the time.

A Cancer woman loves positions and can accept a variety of responsibilities. She can work very well in a relaxed environment. She can make a great writer, singer, actress, painter, teacher or anything else that gives her an opportunity to boost her self-esteem. She can be a great counsellor. She can also do well with fashion products. If she believes that she can make good money in life, she will surely do so. She also keeps in mind that it is necessary to save for difficult times. So, although she is fond of a luxurious life, she is quite judicious in spending money.

Leo

Dates: Hindu Calendar Aug. 14 to Sept. 14	
Element:	Fire
Ruling planet:	Sun
Symbol:	The Lion
Quality:	Fixed, stable
Colour:	Gold, golden brown
Gems:	Amber, *manak*
Best friends:	Aries and Sagittarius
Virtues:	Bravery, loyalty, steadfast in love and everything else
Weaknesses:	Vanity, arrogance, bossy disposition
Celebrities:	Madonna, Neil Armstrong, Bill Clinton, Sir Walter Scott, Fidel Castro, Jacqueline Kennedy-Onassis, Dr S. Radhakrishnan, Napoleon Bonaparte, George Bernard Shaw

Characteristics

A Leo person is easy to identify from his status and looks, as he possesses many remarkable talents. Even when in a quiet mood, he is able to make an impact and leaves a lasting effect on people. Like his ruling sign, he is one of the most important persons of the Zodiac world. A Leo person has great stamina. His energy and endurance often impress others. He leads an exciting life, as he hates a boring life. He always lives to fulfil his dreams. He is often motivated by a clear vision of success. He is quite capable of fulfilling his dreams. It is also true that, at times, a Leo may reach the brink of bankruptcy but he is also able to work his way out of the situation. In that respect, his professional achievements are often great.

Basically, Leo is generous and protective. His chosen woman possesses ideal qualities and he likes to be associated with such a woman only. He is a good natured and life-loving person, and doesn't get angry very often. He is a very strong, honest and dependable person. He definitely likes to be married and most women feel secure in his company. He often exhibits warm and tender feelings towards others.

But Leo has a dark side too. If he sometimes loses his temper he may even disassociate people from his life. He wants most people to obey him and move fast, while he may himself be a lazy Leo. At times he is so frank and outspoken that he becomes intolerable to others. Since he does not like to mince words, he is not a very diplomatic person. A Leo always likes to give advice to others and tell them what to do. He would like to rule the world and loves fame, power and fortune.

The classic Leo is supremely dignified, refusing to do anything mean or low. He tends to be honest and does not indulge in deception. He may be stubborn at times. He is often ambitious, determined and enterprising. He wants to possess the best and do the best. He often seeks an office with that motive only. Thus, he always wants positions of authority. Many Leos like to pursue careers in media, movies, education, and as professional speakers as well as entertainers. Some of the above characteristics are reflected in the given table.

A Leo woman has the courage, pride and grace of a lioness. No one should underestimate her for she can bounce back with agility and recover from any lost ground and failures. When her confidence is intact she has a great sense of dignity and authority. As she is a natural actress, she can play the roles of superstar and goddess. If she possesses most Leo qualities, she emits vitality, enthusiasm and colossal energy. She is often a great organiser, a great leader and loyal to her friends. In case she does not like someone, she can be a great critic.

A Leo woman can be anything and take up any career she chooses. She frequently likes challenging jobs. At times she can create her own positions because she possesses plenty of qualities. A Leo woman mostly enjoys careers in singing, talk shows, teaching, acting and counselling. Any wise and intelligent employer can easily get the best out of her, for she likes to be involved and recognised. She always knows the value of possessing good credits and making intelligent investments.

Table 5

Benefits and Shortcomings of Leo

Characteristics	Advantages	Shortcomings
Ambitious	Develops character persistently	Whimsical/foolhardy
Aristocratic	Distinguished	Stubborn
Authoritative	Opinions are valued	Believes he knows all
Capable	Persistent efforts	Bossy/commanding
Confident	Brave	Show off
Courageous	Faces adversity	Reckless
Determined	Colossal willpower	Obstinate
Energetic	Vigorous	Calm when required
Extravagant	Loves great lifestyle	Bankruptcy
Generous	Ready to help	Mostly likes recognition
Honest	Keeps goal in view	Lacks tactics
Optimistic	Looks at the bright side only	Often behaves foolishly
Organised	Efficient/smart	Mean/petty
Temperamental	Exhibits opinions openly	Showy and dramatic at times

Virgo

Dates:	Hindu Calendar Sept. 15 to Oct. 14
Element:	Earth
Ruling planet:	Mercury
Symbol:	The Virgin
Quality:	Flexibility
Colours:	Orange

Gem:	Agate, *panna*
Best friends:	Capricorn and Taurus
Weaknesses:	Worrying nature, low self-esteem
Celebrities:	Mother Teresa, Michael Jackson, Ingrid Bergman, Peter Sellers, Sophia Loren, Agatha Christie, Amitabh Bachchan, Leo Tolstoy

Characteristics

A Virgo person has many sides of character — complex throughout with mingling viewpoints. It is really difficult to figure out a Virgo as he lives so much through his inner, private being. As he derives a great deal of pleasure from thinking, he thinks about everything and nothing. Because he can spend so much time living on thoughts, analysing them with his unique logic, he seldom forgets to live in the outside world. As he is mostly engaged in thoughts, he loves libraries, likes to indulge in research and computer programming, and is also drawn to system analysis, education, media and handicrafts. He feels extremely happy in such activities.

Often uniquely talented, he is generally unusual in all kinds of ways. Whether a songwriter, performer, actor, homemaker, nurse, or doctor, there is often a whole lot happening within him. With such varied qualities, he can fit himself in most circumstances and places. Virgo is a sign deeply related to communication as Mercury rules it.

One of the downsides of this sign is at times gaining favour from people or falling from grace. Astrologically, a Virgo person is considered to possess great moral values. People expect great purity from him. It is thus quite interesting that many nuns, priests and religious people are often born under Virgo. As he often desires to live as a perfect person, while being good at heart, he likes meditation, prayers and occult practices.

A Virgo person can be quite complicated but keeps trying to be uncomplicated. His efforts at trying to put everything in order don't always work. In some form or another, a Virgo person acts like a perfectionist or a good organiser. It may sometimes lead him to be eccentric because he constantly keeps trying to reach extremes in all walks of life. In fact, a Virgo person is hardworking. As such, he often possesses the ability to be a leader in different professions.

As he loves order, conditions where ritual and routine pervade appeal to him. He possesses a kind heart and may go out of his way to make others happy. One of his greatest strengths is his great sense of discrimination. He likes to test all the new information and keeps organising as he proceeds. But his attitude of discrimination sometimes leads him to be critical and fault finding. Some of the above characteristics are contained in the following table.

Table 6

Benefits and Shortcomings of Virgo

Characteristics	Advantages	Shortcomings
Disciplined	Self-controlled	Not flexible
Discriminating	Appreciates fine work	Critical
Eccentric	Unusual	Often misunderstood
Exacting	Sticks to norms	Perfectionist
Hardworking	Productive	Lazy
Logical	Good reasoning	Emotional
Methodical	Quite efficient	Lacks spontaneity
Modest	Humble	Often overlooked
Quiet	Conspicuous	Keeps to himself
Secretive	Mysterious	Mistrusted
Self-contained	Identifies with self	Distant at times
Worried	Overcautious	Suspicious

A Virgo woman is one of the most talented persons in the world. But her beauty and talents are seldom enough to fulfil her desires. She is on a constant quest to excel. In her romantic dealings she allows herself to become exposed to her man. In fact, no other Zodiac sign tends to give more in relationships with others than a Virgo woman. She can be the most sacrificing of all the Zodiac signs. Once deeply involved in something, she does not like to rest until she reaches the goal. Such qualities serve her well. She is usually hardworking, practical and very modest in seeing her virtues clearly. She is committed to constant betterment and personal development.

She boldly faces her fears. She values facts and information and likes to pursue research to finalise her opinions and views.

She is the most accomplished woman of the Zodiac. She likes to do all jobs to the best of her ability. As she is intelligent, she is a valuable contributor to any company. She tends to be more attracted towards arts, literature, entertainment and publishing. She can make a great sculptor, a passionate writer and a talented actress. She can also be a successful doctor, dentist or nurse.

Libra

Dates:	Hindu Calendar Oct. 15 to Nov. 13
Element:	Air
Ruling planet:	Venus
Symbol:	The Scale
Quality:	Cardinal (activity)
Colours:	Blue, turquoise
Gems:	Diamond, opal
Best friends:	Gemini and Aquarius
Virtues:	Taste for designing
Weaknesses:	Lacks desires and feels helpless
Celebrities:	Mahatma Gandhi, Shammi Kapoor, Hema Malini, Swami Ram Tirth

Characteristics

The symbol of this sign has a deeply symbolic meaning for the Sun sign Libra people. It inspires balance and harmony in people's lives. The Libran needs a harmonious background, free from undue pressure or argument. When confronted with a problem, he waits for matters to resolve themselves rather than take sides.

A Libran does not like loneliness. Complete happiness for him means sharing his life with others. A typical Libran enjoys working in a team and excels at any arbitration. A Libran may sometimes be accused of being lazy but this is not quite true. He does not enjoy dirty jobs, but is certainly not lazy. He may be very romantic. Although usually peace loving, he sometimes provokes arguments to test whether his partner loves him. As a parent, he is kind and loving. He can be a great diplomat. He is very sociable and often idealistic but indecisive too. He is easily influenced to change his opinions. Self-indulgence and flirtation are the weaker sides of his personality.

How and when to make a choice is a constant process of a Libran's existence. But his life is constantly like work in progress. He loves to live a fine life and desires a very happy marriage. He tries to seek great friendships and believes in living in luxury. He generally likes to have a good time. One of his great weaknesses is the inability to say 'No', even when required. Thus, he is indecisive on most occasions. He is often popular with people because he is a natural charmer. He has great power of persuasion and is well liked by others. His polished charms and good appearance are greatly comforting to others. He can be a great entertainer and witty. Blessed with innate wisdom, he can see both sides of most situations. He has a great sense of justice, which his sign already depicts. Some of the above characteristics are reflected in the following table.

Table 7

Benefits and Shortcomings of Libra

Characteristics	Advantages	Shortcomings
Affectionate	Warm-hearted	Can lead people
Appealing	Magnetic charm	Sends out wrong messages
Artistic	Talented	Erratic
Balanced	Stable	Dislikes change
Charming	Alluring	Persuades cunningly
Creative	Inventive	Loaded with too much
Diplomatic	Leads smoothly	Self-ruling
Easygoing	Relaxed	Lazy, with no initiative
Generous	Not selfish	Unwise
Gentle	Soft	Weak-willed
Honourable	Respectful	Swollen head
Just	Fair	Self-determined values
Peaceful	Calm	Quits crucial battles

A **Libra woman** is truly a feminine woman of the Zodiac, but is one of the strongest too. She often possesses a forceful personality and stands out in a crowd. She loves to be creative, designing clothes and decorating houses, etc. She is stylish. The most charming side of her character is to keep her innermost desires secret. She has a charming smile, sincere heart, a strong will and also a stubborn disposition. She is good at pretending and can say 'No' when she really means 'Yes' and vice versa. She can be sensitive, affectionate, and intelligent now, and then do a complete about turn in the next instant. Thus, at times she is childish, self-centred and tactless as well as unreliable. When she's feeling negative, she can become quite complex, restless and argumentative. On such occasions, she can also be irrational. But when her thoughts are positive, she appears to be brilliant in all aspects.

As Venus rules her, she values beauty, justice, harmony and equality. She also expresses those traits through her actions. She loves everything related to nature and beauty. But, above everything else, she loves peace of mind. Many Libran women love music. She is artistic in nature and can make a good career in writing, movies, theatre, interior decoration, law, antiquities, public relations and teaching.

Scorpio

Dates: Hindu Calendar Nov. 14 to Dec. 13	
Element:	Water
Ruling planet:	Pluto, Mars
Symbol:	The Scorpion
Quality:	Stable (fixed)
Colours:	Deep red
Gems:	Topaz, *munga*
Best friends:	Pisces and Cancer
Virtues:	Loyalty, honesty
Weaknesses:	Intolerance, misjudging others
Celebrities:	Pablo Picasso, Bill Gates, Indira Gandhi, Jawaharlal Nehru, Hillary Clinton, Charles Bronson, Prince Charles

Characteristics

A Scorpio mostly likes his boundaries to be intact. He possesses an increasingly sharp intelligence and a wide variety of natural talents. He combines desire, passion and uniqueness. He is intense, powerful and glorious in character. A Scorpio is very powerful. He is born with determination, energy and stubbornness to fulfil his greatest dreams. The powerful ruling planet (Pluto/Mars) provides him with a great number of qualities and characteristics and equip him to overpower life's challenges and obstacles. He does not like to take 'No' for an answer.

A Scorpio loves taking risks and is not disheartened when the chance is lost. He starts with new vigour and strives hard to win. Many Scorpio men are highly successful in life. But when things don't go their way, they are likely to blame themselves and hurt their own selves. One of the hardest things for a Scorpio is to accept that he is not the master of everything.

At times sex can run his life and can make him friendly to some stray people in sexual relationships. His sex appeal is difficult to describe. He may appear reserved and unyielding at times, but he remains tense within. There is an enormous amount of passion within him, waiting to be released. If he desires to lead a happy life, he needs to control that passion or his life will go astray. Only if he controls his passion can his life's path become smooth.

He cannot be compared to anyone in terms of criticising and condemning himself. This kind of thought process is his worst enemy. It is, therefore, very important for him to abandon this attitude that brings him depression and sadness. It is very important for Scorpio to choose the right kind of people in life. It also applies to his choice of the right kind of mate or girl-friend.

Fighting adversities is part of his life. He does not believe in compromise as he has very strong views about life. He has an open disposition and is very frank and clear. He does not mince words. In that respect a Scorpio is quite honest. He never likes to give an opinion that he considers incorrect and inappropriate. It is because of this quality of frankness and honesty that he can easily negotiate deals and contracts, which others can hardly win.

33

Not many Scorpios like change. He likes to keep everything in its chosen place. Being independent in nature, he can be extremely stubborn and strong-willed. He does not like to heed advice, even when it may be beneficial to him. When others do him wrong, he hardly forgives them. Thus, when he removes someone from his life, he does it for good. But he takes such decisions after great thought. It must be noted that a Scorpio's ego is his biggest strength and force of motivation. At the same time, it can be his biggest challenge to stop him doing good to others. A Scorpio has so many other remarkable qualities. He is a perfectionist, hard working, determined, brave, reliable and loyal, with a great capacity to stick to a job. He can focus closely on final details without being distracted. The following table outlines the above qualities and shortcomings of Scorpio.

Table 8

Benefits and Shortcomings of Scorpio

Characteristics	Advantages	Shortcomings
Determined	Strong-willed	Always desires power
Influential	Can persuade	Controlling
Magnetic nature	Influences easily	Trouble-finder
Passionate	Full of desires	Unbridled temper
Powerful	Controls power	Trouble-maker
Quiet	Limited within	Unpleasant thinking
Secretive	Facts not revealed	Single-tracked
Sexy	Seduces effectively	Not truly friendly
Subtle	Tender	Skilful
Unyielding	Strong in opinions	Not flexible

A Scorpio woman has a very powerful, inquiring mind. She is much stronger than the other Zodiac women. She may look very gentle from outside, but she is very firm inside. She is quite self-sufficient and independent by nature. She often keeps her emotions to herself. She is quite successful at home as well as professionally. Among the Zodiac signs, she makes one of the best mothers. At the same time, she is also the most obsessive and possessive person. With such qualities a Scorpio woman is happier in her own company rather than running after men. But she likes men who are stronger than her and superior in intelligence, wealth and power.

A Scorpio woman is inclined towards business. But with her remarkable talents and abilities, she can handle other jobs as well. All that she desires is success. She can be good in running companies. She can also make a good scientist, healer, detective, reporter, as well as a good journalist. She can take up jobs in medical fields and can also be successful in the computer and engineering fields.

Sagittarius

Dates: Hindu Calendar Dec. 14 to Jan. 13	
Element:	Fire
Ruling planet:	Jupiter
Symbol:	The Archer
Quality:	Flexibility
Colours:	Yellow, light blue, cream
Gems:	Turquoise, *pukhraj*
Virtue:	Fearless approach to life, adventurous, positive attitude
Weaknesses:	Stubbornness
Celebrities:	Frank Sinatra, John F. Kennedy Jr., Bruce Lee, Walt Disney, Kirk Douglas, Tina Turner, Jane Fonda, Jane Austen, Atal Bihari Vajpayee

Characteristics

Being born under one of the luckiest Zodiac signs, a Sagittarius person is rich in many ways. He is rich in spirit and true in friendship. He loves to take chances and can go to extremes. He can shock people by his free spirit and unusual decisions. Like the Zodiac symbol, a Sagittarian always aims high. But without a target or goal in mind he may be most ineffective. When he is inspired by his own strong will, he is most loving and effective. He can be quite matchless when he gets down to doing what he loves. It is also true that when out of gear, a Sagittarian is unsettled emotionally, physically and at times spiritually.

The key theme of a Sagittarian is freedom. He likes to attempt transcending the limits that most people accept. He is often involved in quests for spiritual revelation and philosophical engagements. He loves to push back the boundaries of inner and outer space. Liberty is the Sagittarian's rallying cry and he likes to take great responsibilities. Like his symbol, he is straightforward in manner. He possesses great love for nature. Like the Archer symbol that represents his Zodiac sign, a Sagittarian aims very high. He may lose faith in his own luck or results, but that does not keep him down for long. He restarts, reorganises himself and aims again to attain his best. He is always curious, especially about the mysteries of life. By disposition, birth and inclination he is religious and often thinks about god. Overall, he has great confidence in himself. He is very inquisitive and wants to know everything that there is to know under the sun. Other people always fascinate him. He is a good conversationalist and can engage in a discussion with most people, young, old or of any religion.

As time passes, he develops somewhat philosophical qualities, with which he inspires others. Restlessness is his major fault but he can overcome it. Career-wise, there is plenty of scope for a Sagittarian. He enjoys publishing and is happy in the field of higher education. He would be very happy to work abroad. He can be a good veterinary doctor and can take law and church/temple (worship) as his profession. Primarily, he loves freedom of expression. He always likes to have meaningful relationships with people. He has a great sense of fun and is very enthusiastic.

Since he hates leading a boring life, he quickly fills his life with activities such as attending and participating in dramas, making plans, projects, and other activities. He is not much concerned with success or failure as much he likes to go on to the next step in life, where he meets excitement and thrill. Relationships, friendships, love and passion are the foundations of his life and mean a great deal to him. Most of these qualities are reflected in the table.

Table 9

Benefits and Shortcomings of Sagittarius

Characteristics	Advantages	Shortcomings
Adaptability	Good spirited	Not quite reliable
Ambitious	Thinks a lot	An extremist
Athletic	Quite healthy	Keeps good health
Candid	Honest	May hurt feelings
Confident	Self-confident	Arrogant
Egocentric	Self-centred	Show off
Energetic	Great strength	Overactive
Enthusiastic	Desire to improve	Thinks loosely at times
Generous	Bestows kindness	Negative thinker
Impatient	Eager	Gets into problems
Intelligent	Thinks freely	Thoughts are not quite aligned
Impulsive	Spontaneous	Not adhering to reason
Logical	Learns a lot	Broods too often
Optimistic	Thinks positively	Unrealistic
Persuasive	Influential	Often uses force
Philosophical	Independent thinker	Easily influenced
Restless	Has lots of energy	Doesn't stay calm
Reckless	Bold	Often courts danger

A **Sagittarius woman** is often powerful in a fundamental manner. She has very strong ideas about what she desires. She can fight to attain her own and others' peace. Her qualities are many. She can sometimes tap dance, wind surf, ski and be a great sportswoman. With such qualities and varied interests, she is an ambitious idealist who believes that she has great responsibilities to make a difference wherever she lives.

She often has a mission in life. She is outspoken, confident and impatient. She places a high value on truth and sincere affection. She is god-oriented. Without any aim or inspiration in life, she is likely to suffer from melancholy and depression. She loves movies and likes to go out to dinner with friends. She likes dancing, playing or watching games. Most Sagittarian women are nature lovers. She likes camping, hiking, riding and even rock climbing. She is very caring and loyal to friends. She can listen well and speak very affectionately.

She is ambitious and hard working. She can do her best as a lawyer, a performer, a teacher, a stylist, in the beauty industry, in literature, in travel-oriented jobs, and journalism as well. She is a good student, often opting for higher education. She can excel in sports, archaeology and science. She is also good at public relations and education.

Capricorn

Dates: Hindu Calendar Jan. 14 to Feb. 13	
Element:	Earth
Ruling planet:	Saturn
Symbol:	The Goat
Quality:	Essential (activity)
Colours:	Green and black
Gems:	Moonstone, *neelam*
Good friends:	Taurus and Virgo
Virtues:	Discipline, consistency and organisational skills
Weaknesses:	Unforgiving of others, takes life too seriously
Celebrities:	Anthony Hopkins, Rudyard Kipling, Muhammad Ali, Aristotle Onassis, Ava Gardner, Cary Grant

Characteristics

A Capricorn person is like a goat, surefooted and able to negotiate everything with great care and responsibility. He has a great deal of determination. He examines every decision and opportunity very carefully to minimise risks. He is cautious, serious, methodical, realistic, and determined to reach the very top of his abilities. He is capable of sacrifice and endurance as well. A Capricorn's planning and endurance are qualities necessary for his upward journey in life. But he has weaknesses too. Sometimes he may develop a hopeless, negative attitude and may often feel that there is so much going against him. But he also has many good qualities. He has a great sense of humour, which is often unusual. His witty remarks may astound and delight all at the same time.

Such persons don't have to do much with emotions and tend towards being cool in love. But once committed, he is tremendously loyal. He has great power of concentration. He doesn't believe in shortcuts. He has considerable pride and possesses inherent ambition to move up the social ladder. He desires to improve other people. A Capricorn can often make a good athlete. His weaknesses are knees, teeth, skin and bones, which are vulnerable.

In fact, a Capricorn has a huge list of useful personality traits to help him and others. His best characteristics are patience, perseverance, independence, determination and firmness, which come to him naturally. He learns quickly and can go quite deep into the areas of knowledge he thinks or likes best. He has the vision, power and grit to make it to the top. If necessary, he can do it all alone.

Capricorn falls quite distinctly into three types. The first group is aligned with the mountain goat – charged with ambition and aiming to climb as high up the mountain as possible. The second type is aligned with the docile garden goat, which is not much interested in climbing either the mountain or the ladder of success. He seeks less challenging routines and is happy to stay on solid ground. Sometimes, this kind of Capricorn likes to live in the same town forever. The third type is a combination of the two. Such a person likes to blow hot and cold when it comes to fulfilling his dreams and ambitions. One can easily observe this in his attitude, behaviour and focus in relation to his speed, style and way of living, as well as the pursuit of goals.

The basic truth about Capricorns is that most of them tend to switch back and forth between a fast and slow pace of life. Therefore, he works hard all week and then withdraws to a country retreat for a break to enjoy the weekend happily. Many Capricornians put great efforts to secure tomorrow and build the future of their dreams. Truly speaking he is one of the most determined and organised persons in the Zodiac. At his best, he can handle many tasks simultaneously. As he possesses many talents, he is quite capable of building the ladder that he eventually uses to climb to success. Friends, romance and family mean a great deal for the Capricorn man. He can make a great contribution and difference to the world around him in varied ways. Some become famous, while others make a difference by working behind the scenes. Amazingly, the Capricorn man is not a perfectionist. However, even when things are going right for him, he often wishes they were better. Some of the above qualities are contained in the following table.

Table 10

Benefits and Shortcomings of Capricorn

Characteristics	Advantages	Shortcomings
Ambitious	Has goals	Dislikes relaxing
Admired	Most appreciated	Falls down from the top
Caring	Keeps friends in mind	Overprotective
Clever	Defensive reasoning	Sarcastic at times
Critical	Likes details	Observes faults smartly
Cautious	Trustworthy	Uncertain of things
Determined	Patient	Can go on without gains
Goal-oriented	Has a mission	Often thinks of the future
Honest	Trustworthy	Only tries to be honest
Melancholy	Looks inwards persistently	Totally depressed
Powerful	Great leader	Bossy to an extent
Practical	Good in action	Can't fulfil desires
Sensible	Has good ideas	Old-fashioned
Stubborn	Likes old routine	Deliberately falls in a ditch

A Capricorn woman can be seen in a variety of physical shapes, such as frail, robust or a mixed type, but she is a dynamic person. She is sublime, quick thinking, talented, compassionate and caring. She is often a good mother, sister, friend or wife. She is extremely feminine and has a great sense of style. She possesses great sincerity and subconsciously moves towards her goals. At times, she is also admired for her extraordinary wit. She is quite diplomatic and can smile sweetly when others may be on the brink of rage. She is well aware of the problems and hardships that she may have to face on the path to success. She leaves no stone unturned to reach her goal. She is a great friend to those who are her cosmic friends.

She is often not very tolerant. But with her children and family she cultivates tolerance. She is quite serious by nature. She is usually not extravagant in terms of clothes. She is self-conscious about her form and can do a great deal to look her best. With her, time is always at a premium and she is often in a hurry. She likes to work for charities and takes great interest in the welfare of other people. Many Capricorn women are multi-talented. She can have more than one career at a time. She can often make a good writer, journalist, professional speaker, artist, musician, professional athlete, golfer, gymnast, and a good public relations and human affairs person.

Aquarius

Dates: Hindu Calendar Feb. 14 to March 13	
Element:	Air
Ruling planet:	Uranus (Saturn)
Symbol:	The Water Bearer
Quality:	Fixed (stability)
Colours:	Electric blue, black
Gems:	Sapphire, Opal, *neelam*
Best friends:	Gemini, Libra
Virtues:	Reliability, bright vision of the future
Weaknesses:	Emotional loneliness, fear of rejection
Celebrities:	Paul Newman, Charles Dickens, Prince Andrew, Athina Onassis, Ronald Reagan, Linda Blair, Thomas Edison

Characteristics

An Aquarian is quite outstanding in his uniqueness. He is generally a creative type. In fact, life would be easier for an Aquarian if he is able to understand his own nature, which is quite different from persons born under other Zodiac signs. As his way of thinking is different from persons of other signs, he is likely to be misunderstood. There will be occasions when his different attitude towards life will startle people. Since an Aquarian works according to his own whims and fancies, he is likely to lead an exceptional life – different from others in matters of social customs, religious rituals, etc. He is extremely good at heart.

An Aquarian will never betray his friends, even if they betray him. It makes him a great friend. He doesn't go by schedules or make any plans to lead him too far. On account of certain responsibilities, if he has to yield too much to the schedule, it makes him physically unwell. He is then depressed and restless. As the sign needs more activity than the other signs of the Zodiac, an Aquarian breaks away from the routine. It is to his great advantage that an Aquarian has an inventive mind. Since he attacks a problem from many different angles, he is often able to solve it. The ruling planet of Aquarius is Uranus (Saturn as well), which rules electricity. Therefore, it is no wonder that Thomas Edison, an Aquarian, invented electricity. At times, he has so much going on in his mind that he may lose track of the main destination or plan. His ability to focus helps him overcome any distractions that he might face on the way. He has great insight into most matters he deals with. But an Aquarian must remember that while too much thinking may be an asset, it can also break him. It is therefore very important for him to lighten up and open up to others.

Too many thoughts can also make him neurotic. It is because of the nature of the Aquarian that he lives through his thoughts rather than the reality of life. This is applicable to his romantic life too. As he continuously involves himself with thinking and analysing, it often works as an impediment to the deeper, heartfelt connection of true love. Therefore, to be successful in love, he needs to live in the real world. It is very important for an Aquarian to be more practical than thought-oriented if he desires to lead a happy life. Uranus leads to genius thinking, technology and scientific breakthroughs. It also rules inspiration and higher cosmic connections. To be a potentially creative genius, an Aquarian must be action-oriented rather than totally mind-oriented. An Aquarian is a social reformer who expects everyone to conform to his specific perception for their own good. The following table displays most of the qualities at a glance.

Table 11

Benefits and Shortcomings of Aquarius

Characteristics	Advantages	Shortcomings
Analytical	Good thinking process	Distracted easily
Assertive	Responsible	Single-tracked
Detached	Free thinker	Prone to accidents
Eccentric	Unique personality	Out of step
Genius	Bright thoughts	Misunderstood
Honest	Humble	Astonishing
Humane	Kind	Exploited
Independent	Self-sufficient	Doesn't accept advice
Innovative	New ways	Persistent
Inventive	Creative thinking	Ahead of time
Original	Creative	Mocked at
Patient	Composed	Represses sadness
Progressive	Possesses clear vision	Confused
Tolerant	Understanding	Taken advantage of
Unbiased	Impartial	Hypocritical

An Aquarius woman has a unique feminine magic within her, which can be dazzling to behold. She is not an easy woman to know in many ways. She has a wide range of interests and values. She loves freedom above all things and is comfortable with all levels of people in society. She is sweet and charming but, at times, quite distant. Sometimes she is unpredictable and can surprise or even shock anyone who thinks he knows her well. She may act friendly one moment, seemingly seductive and appealing, but the very next moment she may give the feeling that she doesn't even know you.

An Aquarian woman often loves a good cause. At times the cause may be to save the homeless, or to build an orphanage. She will do her best to help such people. She wants to serve the world at large, rather than her own satisfaction. She has an inborn tendency to do things her way. She knows many different ways to reach her goal. Therefore, she may choose different careers in life. She may work as a freelance artist, writer, photographer, consultant, run an antique shop, work for art galleries, or even in a bakery.

An Aquarian woman may be quite happy to have her own business because it suits her independent nature. She can also be a scientist, inventor or researcher. She can also pursue some kind of social work or counselling. Acting, comedy and even singing may appeal to her. She doesn't like to pursue a job merely for the sake of money, but for her interests and beliefs. She is happiest when able to fulfil her ideas.

Pisces

Dates: Hindu Calendar March 14 to April 13	
Element:	Water
Ruling planet:	Neptune (Jupiter)
Symbol:	The Fish
Quality:	Flexibility
Colours:	Green, yellow
Gems:	Moonstone, *pukhraj*
Virtues:	Adaptability, intuition
Weaknesses:	Oversensitive, lack of faith in the future
Celebrities:	Elizabeth Taylor, Albert Einstein, Jerry Lewis, Edward Kennedy, Chelsea Clinton, Michael Chang, Chuck Norris

Characteristics

In fact, the sign Pisces rules the sixth sense, dreams and illusions. Therefore, the hidden realms affect Pisceans the most. A Piscean will usually spend most of his time in his own innermost, private world. A Piscean will be most happy to live in places like beach huts, log cabins, on boats or trailers. He enjoys hiking, skiing, swimming, surfing and even walking along the seashore. He can also indulge in drinking – an unwise and unhealthy pursuit. As the sign indicates, many Pisceans are beach lovers, boat owners, fishermen, and beach lifeguards too.

When influenced most by this sign, a Piscean will be able to draw other people towards him. He then makes new friends because people see something different in him. But even then he can feel lonely, which makes his existence complicated and difficult. He is truly a romantic person. Being adventurous, romance means a lot to him. But if there is a failure or break in love, he undergoes a major heartbreak. And he recovers only when there is another love in his life. Then the broken heart mends magically. There is nothing so great in the life of a Piscean than a new romance.

One cannot get to know a Piscean so easily. His physical appearance can be misleading and his dress can be a total contradiction of his personality. He can be a very pleasant colleague, willing to make sacrifices for others. He is well intentioned, but lazy. He can be very logical at one time and extremely irrational at another. His moods, behaviour and attitude are not very consistent. So also is his choice of careers. His incredible vision and insight, talent and creativity may lead him to become a poet, sculptor, inventor, musician, designer, movie star, innovator, and even fashion designer. Some of his qualities are listed in the following table.

Table 12

Benefits and Shortcomings of Pisces

Characteristics	Advantages	Shortcomings
Adaptable	Accepts change	Unsteady
Attractive	Has friends	Can lead people on
Compassionate	Concerned, honest	Involved in others' troubles
Creative	Imaginative	Works on ideas without result
Emotional	Deep feelings	Artificial
Gentle	Comforting presence	Defenceless
Graceful	Coordinated	Delicate
Humorous	Open-hearted	Hides failures
Intuitive	Strong cosmic connections	Overtly suspicious

Characteristics	Advantages	Shortcomings
Kind	Generous	Easygoing
Lovable	Warm-hearted	Causes jealousy
Melancholy	Deep feelings	Doleful
Scattered	Wide interests	Absent-minded
Talented	Bestowed with special gifts	Impractical
Understanding	Compassionate	Easily hurt

A Piscean woman is easy to recognise as she often has large eyes. She may not be as good looking but she is still appealing. She can be quite hypnotic in the way she deals with others. When she wants to send a message, she can do so on the mind level and in actuality too. She is usually successful in making her point and getting her message across. In love, romance or sex, she can truly allure men and appear very attractive. She usually succeeds in her designs and can send the right message. Yet, at times, she lacks confidence. She likes to deliver. She can be great and exceptionally successful in life but still wants more.

Whether a housewife, student or businesswoman, she often has her own style. The image she creates before others is unique. She likes to be her own original production. When she wants to fulfil her desires and dreams she is more intuitive, mystical and imaginative than practical. At times she can be extremely contrary to her beliefs and ideas. Although she cares about others, sometimes she may give a different impression outwardly. As she is extremely versatile, she can choose almost any career. She is often attracted to the arts. She can be a fashion designer, a good singer, an actress, and a doctor. She likes to work with the people who are really bright and appealing.

Chapter Two

The Basics of Astrology

It is very important to properly understand the 12 signs of the Zodiac, indicated in the beginning of the first chapter along with the birth dates. Without this it will not be possible for the reader to learn, read or understand one's horoscope. In fact, it is not very difficult to cast a horoscope if you can understand the basics. What are those basics and what simple procedures does one need to cast it? This is explained in a simple manner in the current chapter.

The important basics revolve around the knowledge of the 'meaning attributed to each house' and the meaning of the rising sign in the first house or the ascendant. With this, it is also imperative to understand how the rising sign is ascertained. First, let's begin with the rising sign. All this information will enable you to cast a new chart when needed. But before you learn to cast a chart, you must know the characteristics connected to each house. And, it is also necessary to learn what quality each rising sign bestows on an individual. *If you read the chapter on the Basics thoroughly, you can easily learn to cast a chart (kundali).*

The Rising Sign

In order to cast a horoscope, it is important for the astrologer to know some crucial details, like the place, date and time of one's birth. On the basis of the time of birth, with the help of an already made out astrological Indian calendar or *Panchang** (refer to *Appendix 1*), an astrologer can calculate and find out which, out of the 12 Zodiac signs, is rising in the horizon at the time of the child's birth. This sign occupies the first house, or the ascendant, in a horoscope and is known as **the rising sign**. In 24 hours of a day, each of the 12 signs of the Zodiac rises once, roughly for two hours each, to complete the cycle of the day.

According to the English or other astrological calendars, the Sun remains in a sign for almost one month. After a month when it enters the next sign, on the first day the same Zodiac sign also rises with it and stays in the horizon for almost two hours. It goes on like this until the day is over. Then the same cycle starts all over again. Therefore, you must understand clearly that there is a deep relationship between the rising sign and the Sun's rising in a sign in the eastern horizon.

Yet they are two separate aspects of astrology. The first step is to cast a chart (*kundali*). It can easily be done with the help of the *Panchang*, in which you will find monthly charts starting from January to December, containing the starting time of each sign (*lagna* or *rashi*) on each day, until the end of a month (please see *Appendix 1*). This will help you in determining the rising sign for a new chart (newly born baby). When the next sign starts on the same day, it is also the end of the previous sign. A careful study of the *Panchang* will easily enable you to find out **the rising sign** on any day over 12 months. The rest of the chart can be prepared with the help of the calendar (*Panchang*), which is self-explanatory. Let us explain it in more detail to further clarify our point.

To find out which rising sign should occupy the ascendant in a horoscope at the time of a person's birth can be understood with the help of an example. According to the Hindu calendar, *Panchang*, let's say the Sun rises in Aries in the east, roughly at 6 a.m. on 14 April. At the time of the rising of the Sun, the sign Aries also rises with it and stays in that sign for roughly two hours, i.e., until 8 a.m. After that, the sign Taurus rises for the next two hours. But the Sun keeps travelling in Aries until 13 May.

Let's clarify this issue further through a concrete example. If one is born at 4.22 a.m. on 3 March, his rising sign should be Capricorn. But how did we reach the conclusion that at 4.22 a.m. the sign Capricorn was rising? In order to find out which sign is rising at a particular time, it is necessary to first know the time of the Sun's rising in the horizon on that particular day. So, on 3 March, if the Sun rose in the horizon at 7.06 a.m. in Aquarius, the rising sign Aquarius will approximately stay in the horizon for another 38 minutes that day, after the Sun has risen. Thereafter, the sign Pisces will take over for roughly two hours. But the Sun continues rotating in Aquarius for the remaining days, until it enters the sign Pisces on 14 March, as already indicated at the beginning of the first chapter (*see Table A*).

In fact, from 14 February to 2 March (Hindu calendar), the Sun has already travelled in the sign Aquarius for 17 days. Thus, 17 multiplied by 4 (minutes) makes it 1 hour and 8 minutes.** This means that though the Sun rose in the sign Aquarius on 3 March at 7.06 a.m., Aquarius had already appeared in the horizon an hour and 22 minutes earlier. So, on 3 March the sign Aquarius rose in the horizon at 5.44 a.m. and stayed in the same sign until 7.44 a.m. Thus, the sign Capricorn rose in the horizon on 3 March around 3.44 a.m. and stayed until 5.43 a.m.. So, at 4.22 a.m. Capricorn was rising, though it stayed in that sign for a few minutes only.

The following birth chart is presented for the benefit of readers to show how the 12 signs are allocated in the houses in a chart (*kundali*). A person (*jatak*) born at 4.22 a.m. on 3 March, 1962 will have the following chart cast for him. We have not placed the planets in the chart to avoid confusion at this point. The planets will be placed in it at the appropriate time, when other important information relating to a horoscope is given to the reader. The number(s) mentioned with the sign(s) indicates the number that astrologers have traditionally assigned to that particular sign (symbol). The details are given in the table, presented immediately after the following birth chart.

Birth Chart (*Kundali*) at 4.22 a.m. on 3 March 1962

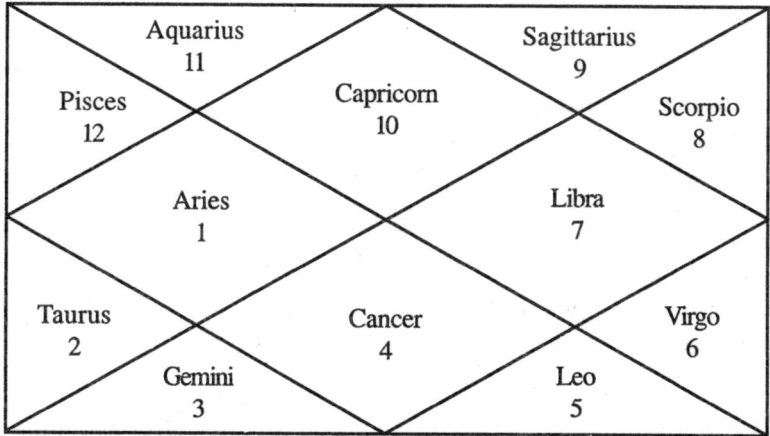

Mathematical Numbers Assigned to Symbols (Signs)

Astrological Signs	Mathematical Number Associated
Aries	1
Taurus	2
Gemini	3
Cancer	4
Leo	5
Virgo	6
Libra	7
Scorpio	8
Sagittarius	9
Capricorn	10
Aquarius	11
Pisces	12

Normally astrologers don't write the name of the symbol or sign in a chart along with the planet, indicating which sign the planet has risen in the chart. The symbol or the sign is indicated by the corresponding mathematical number given above.

The Ascendant

It is necessary to say a few more words about 'the ascendant', which is the most important angle (place) in one's chart. It is also known as **the rising sign**. It is not a planet. It is the sign of the Zodiac belt that was on the eastern horizon of the sky at the time of one's birth. Depending on the rising sign in the ascendant at the time of one's birth, the counting of the subsequent numbers starts from the ascendant in an anti-clockwise direction. This has been pointed out earlier as well. The rising sign rules the person's outward personality, which is what others get to see before they get to know him better.

While explaining how the rising sign is calculated or identified to be placed in it, we have already defined a few things about the ascendant. The reader must keep in mind that the sign occupying the ascendant is absolutely important from an astrological point of view. It reflects the individual's entire personality and his qualities. If any beneficial planets are placed in it, it enhances the power of those planets and also the houses which they govern in the chart. For example, if a benefic Jupiter is placed in the ascendant and controls the fourth and the seventh houses, those houses will be absolutely powerful and bring good results, relating to those houses, for the native throughout life. To elucidate this point, more examples of this kind will be presented to the reader in the fourth chapter of the book. Let us now discuss the characteristics associated with the houses of a chart at this point.

The Houses

Just as the Zodiac is divided into 12 constellations, the same 12-part division is used to allocate the so-called houses. The 30-degree sections of the sky rise above the horizon at two-hour intervals. The houses are numbered, starting at the horizon at the time of a person's birth. Perhaps the idea of this kind of division began with the ancient Egyptians, but later on a Roman astrologer named Manilius popularised the concept of houses.

The first house is the section occupied by the rising sign at the time of the birth of an individual. The remaining houses are numbered in an anti-clockwise manner around the chart. The relationship of the houses is based on the perfect triangle, a sacred symbol in most religions and astrology from ancient times. If we draw such an equal-sided triangle within a circle or a rectangle starting with number 1, the other two points of the triangle will touch houses 5 and 9. For example,

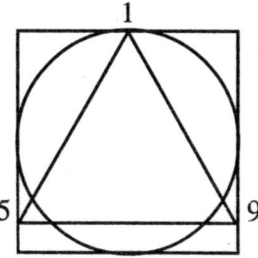

These three houses are said to be *individual* and relate to the self, which includes man's body, emotions, and spirit. Similarly, a

second triangle, with house number 2, will touch houses 6 and 10. These houses are designated *temporal* and influence man's possessions, comforts and honours. The third triangle starts with house number 3. It will touch 7 and 11 and is said to be *relative.* These houses govern man's relationships with others in the form of family, travel, marriage and partnership and friendships. Yet there can be one more triangle which starts with house number 4 and touches houses 8 and 12. It is called *terminal.* These houses concern endings – final conditions, death and limitations.

The houses of an astrological chart are classified into three groups out of 12 houses. They are known as: Angular houses, which are the first, fourth, seventh and the tenth; the Succedent houses, the second, fifth, eighth and eleventh; and, Cadent houses, which are the third, sixth, ninth and twelfth houses. Traditionally, Cadent houses have been referred to as mental houses, although this attribution applies best to the third and ninth houses (the 'lower' and 'higher' mind). In classical astrology, Cadent houses were considered the least powerful houses, in which planets could be posted, and Angular houses were the most powerful. But modern astrologers reckon that the planets placed in Angular houses have the most powerful influence on the outer aspects of a person's life. The planets placed in Cadent houses, they believe, have the most impact on a person's inner life. The rest of the houses exert medium influence on one's inner and outer lives.

From the traditional astrological point of view the most influential houses are the first, ninth, tenth, fifth, fourth and seventh. The third house becomes beneficial only if its owner is placed in a benefic house and sign as well. If the owner of the ninth house sits in it, it becomes highly beneficial on account of the planet's aspect on the ninth house. Now it will be appropriate to present the reader with the qualities or characteristics each house contains, and its impact on an individual. The reader must have this information before any other, as it is the first step to comprehend the nature and meaning of a horoscope. There is a slight difference in the English and the Indian way of counting the houses in a horoscope. From the English point of view, counting of the houses starts clockwise, while from the Indian (Hindu) astrological point of view it starts in an anti-clockwise manner. We shall proceed anti-clockwise, describing the qualities of each house.

The First House

The first house in a chart or a horoscope is also known as the ascendant. This is the house of the self, the place where one's personality and self-image reside. Here one will find one's personal style, mannerisms, temperament, disposition and likes and dislikes. It will also provide the key to why one looks the way one does. It deals with one's childhood and also includes the physical body and is closely tied to health. Coming back to the example of a person born on 3 March, when the ascendant is Aquarius, which bears number 10, if we start counting anti-clockwise, the next house will be occupied by Aquarius and will have number 11. Thus, the counting of each house will proceed while defining their characteristics.

The first house or the ascendant is one of the most important houses in a horoscope. It unfolds one's total personality, complexion, stature, way of thinking, even gait, agility, whether optimistic or pessimistic, dashing or mild, etc. It may take some characteristics from its rising sign as well as from the planet governing that sign, or from the planet(s) sitting in it. In view of this, the characteristics mentioned above will also be affected. For example, a person born on 3 March will have most of the characteristics from the sign Capricorn, also from Saturn and its placement in the chart. Thus, if Saturn is also placed in Capricorn in the horoscope of a person born with Capricorn as the rising sign, he will be down-to-earth, very practical, sometimes doleful, and dashing, etc. The main characteristics of the first house in a nutshell are: the appearance of the native, disposition, outlook on life, carriage, capacity for self-development, vitality, health, inherent strength and physical condition, mental and emotional qualities.

The Second House

Normally the second house is considered the house of speech, wealth and benefits that are all earned by the person himself. It is also related to one's family. It is considered important in calculating one's total lifespan as well. This house is really important as it is the only house that unfolds how a person will earn his living and how much wealth he will acquire during his life. It does not deal with any sudden or unexpected gains in life, which the eleventh house does. In case the planet controlling the second house (also

53

known as the owner of the second house) is placed in a good house, say for example in the 4th, 5th, 9th, 10th or 11th house, the person (*jatak*) will enjoy most of the predicted benefits in relation to this house. It also reveals details about the native's heredity and social background, financial standing, movable possessions, gain and loss of income, personal debts and the manner in which money is acquired.

The Third House

Like the second house, the third house also unfolds a number of boons for a person. It discloses whether the native (*jatak*) will have brothers or sisters. If he has, then how many brothers or sisters will survive. It also tells whether the native will have a good relationship with them; it indicates whether the native will have friends and what types of friends he will have. The most important characteristics of this house is to disclose whether the native will be successful or just waste his time in life. It is the house which tells about the native's character in terms of actions he takes in life to earn his livelihood and to support his family. If the honour of the third house is placed in a good house, like the 1st, 4th, 5th 7th, 9th, 10th or 11th house, the native will enjoy all the aforesaid benefits.

According to some astrologers, this house also indicates the power of mind, dexterity, cleverness, education, short journeys, near relatives, neighbours, immediate environment, writing, communication and lecturing skills.

The Fourth House

Like the third house, the fourth is also characterised by various qualities and benefits that it can bestow upon the *jatak,* if it is placed with a good sign and if its owner is well placed. For example, if Sagittarius is rising in the first house, the fourth house will be occupied by Pisces, which is also controlled by Jupiter. And if Jupiter is not placed in the 6th or 8th or 12th house, the native will enjoy all the benefits attached to the fourth house.

This house indicates the kind of relationship one may have with his mother. It also suggests whether he will have property and land, and what benefits he might have from the property and houses that he builds during his lifetime. It discloses whether he will have any motor vehicle or personal transport and enjoy the services of servants. It also conveys the direction (north, south, east or west) in which the native will ultimately find his destination and finally live. It provides an overall indication of whether the person will lead a happy life. The house generally deals with home and domestic affairs, residence, private affairs, old age, early home life, etc.

The Fifth House

Like the previous four houses, the fifth house is also very important for the native and unfolds a number of benefits for him if its owner is placed in a good house. For example, if Capricorn is rising in this house and its owner Saturn is in its own house (5th), or in the ascendant, the native will enjoy all the benefits from it. He will have a number of good sons—not less than four, who will be well educated and well placed in life. He may produce good writing material that may bring him name and fame.

In fact, this house discloses whether the native will have good education in life, whether he will be able to produce popular writing material; it indicates whether the native is intelligent and has a good relationship with his children, etc. It also indicates how many of his children will live, his wife's miscarriages, etc. But if the owner of this house is not well placed, the native will not enjoy such benefits. This house is mainly related to offsprings, creative and productive urges, recreation, games, leisure, artistic efforts, romantic affairs, speculation, acting, theatre, etc. In case the Sun is in Leo and is placed in this house, the native will enjoy most of its benefits. Traditionally, it is the house of creativity, children, risk-taking, romance and investments.

The Sixth House

It is considered quite a good house in the chart as it pinpoints one's enemies and whether one will suffer from ill-health. Since its natural owner is Mercury, it leads to quick changes in circumstances relating to one's health, illness, impediments (enemies) and relationship with the maternal uncle (mother's brother). In certain countries, especially in Asia, the role of the maternal uncle is great as far as helping the native is concerned. So if this house is well placed (that is, if the rising sign in this house is beneficial and powerful), the native will have all the positive benefits from it. If not, matters of health, and relationship with his/her maternal uncle may be in jeopardy. Some astrologers hold that this house governs food, clothing, pets, capacity to serve, health, diseases, daily work, servants, diet and hygiene, etc. It is also called the house of service and health, working for others, skills.

The Seventh House

This house has a lot in store for the native in terms of benefits, if the owner of the house is well placed. This house tells about the relationship with one's partner (wife/husband), native's marital status, number of girl- or boyfriends he/she will have, quality and talents of the partner, happy or unhappy marriage, sometimes foreign travel, benefits (financial or material) from wife/husband, the support one gets in life from the partner, etc. One can enjoy all these benefits if the house has a good rising sign in it. For example, if the owner of the rising sign of this house is either Mercury, Moon, Jupiter or even Venus, and is placed in the 1st, 3rd, 4th, 5th, 9th, 10th, or 11th house, benefits to the native will be major. But if its owner is placed in the 6th, 8th or 12th house, it may lead to losses.

If the rising sign in the seventh house is Cancer and if its owner Moon is well placed in the chart, the native will have all the benefits from it. Rishi Parashar (the highly learned ancient sage) holds that, in conjunction with the owner of the 2nd house, this house also works as the *markesh,* which means death or indicating death of the native in a particular period. This house is mainly concerned with an individual's partnership, cooperation, marriage, legal contracts, divorce and treaties, etc. It also indicates important friends, associates, legal affairs and business partnerships.

The Eighth House

In comparison to the other houses of the chart, this house reflects many unusual characteristics. It's the only house indicating conditions and circumstances that could bring death. It can indicate the time of accident(s), unusual events leading to death-like situations, serious illness, travel, benefit of hidden wealth, longevity and shortness of life. Benefits from lottery and the native's interest in spiritual matters can also be predicted by the position and strength of this house. In case the owner (planet) of this house is placed in the seventh house, which is the 12th house from it, during the period of that planet the native may suffer death-like pangs, or the person may even die. But if its owner is placed in the 12th or 6th house, it may help in keeping the *jatak* healthy and bestow long life.

The great Rishi Parashar holds that if Saturn sits in the eighth house in its own sign, or in a friendly sign, the native will have quite a long life without many ailments. Saturn bestows aspects of three houses from the house it occupies. For example, if Saturn is sitting in the 6th house, it will have aspects on the third (eighth), seventh (twelfth) and the tenth (third) houses from its position. This means it will look at the 8th, 12th and 3rd houses. In such a case, it fortifies the native's life for good. It is also known as the 'mystical' house, as it deals with death and regeneration. The eighth house is mainly related to birth, death, sexual instincts, sometimes occultism, legacies, benefits from other's property, investigation and afterlife.

The Ninth House

It is one of the most important houses of the chart as it contains many benefits for the native, if the house and its owner are well placed. It deals with everything, from higher education and philosophy to religion. It is the house of mental exploration and long journeys over water, patterns of behaviour and how one can improve them by breaking one's conditioning. The ninth house is also known as one's mental 'model of the universe'. If it is successfully navigated, it can become the place where one can make room in one's life for miracles. It helps in publicly conveying one's ideas and beliefs. It is also related to publishing and teaching. It is the house of the higher mind and exploration, especially philosophical subjects. If well placed, it also helps in possessing greater understanding of life.

The ninth house unfolds how much luck it promises to the native. It deals with overseas travels, and any other fruitful journey. It deals with religious activities. It either always brings good luck, or none at all. It does not provide any luck to a native if in his/her chart its owner is placed in the 12th house, known as the house of waste. It is the house that inspires journeys to religious destinations. In case the owner of this house is placed in the 10th, 11th, 1st, 2nd, 3rd, 4th, 5th, 7th, or 9th house, the strength of this house increases, more so if it is placed in the 10th, 11th, 1st or 3rd house.

Some astrologers believe that the house concerns philosophical interests of the native, religion, law, travel, exploration, research, foreign lands or people and higher education.

The Tenth House

It is the house of *karma* or action that the native will commit during his/her lifetime. It reflects what kind of job one would like to take in life and what shall be his stature in terms of status and money. It deals with one's reputation and career, profession, standing in the community, social role and even what others think about the native. Some call it the house of ambition, attainment and success through one's own efforts. The strength of this house increases if the owner of this house is well placed. For example, if its owner is placed in the 9th, 1st, 3rd, 4th or 5th house, its strength is likely to increase and it will only bring good results.

Its strength also depends on the planet that owns this house. If Mars, Jupiter, Saturn, Venus or Mercury is the owner of this house, its strength and benefits will be enjoyed by the native accordingly. If its owner is coupled with the owner of the 9th house, and is sitting in the 9th, 10th, 11th, 1st, 4th, or even 5th house, it will bring major gains to the native, which could range from great wealth and position in society and government jobs to being a big industrialist. But its placement in bad houses like the 12th, 6th or 8th, and accompanied by bad or inimical planets, could ruin the life of the native and reduce benefits to a great extent. It is mainly concerned with personal image, authority, honour, prestige, career, ambition, father, rulers and employers.

The Eleventh House

Traditionally, this house deals with one's involvement with groups, friends, hopes, long-term dreams and goals. It mainly indicates unexpected or sudden gains in life. Such gains may be on account of a lottery, job, parental position, etc. If this house is strong in the chart, the native will never be short of money in life. In fact, if the owner of this house is coupled with the owner of the second house, and sits either in the second or the eleventh house, it is known as the *Laxmi Yoga* (a great beneficial combination), reflecting the highest benefits wealth-wise. If the owner of this house is Venus and if it sits in the first house, along with the owner of the second house, which is either Mercury or Saturn, it brings great financial benefits to the native from early childhood.

But if the owner of this house sits in the 6th, 8th or 12th house, the native will not enjoy any such gains in life. On the contrary, the person may lose any chances of such benefits from an early age, on account of the death of a parent(s), or some other reason.

This house can also be greatly beneficial if the owner of the first house or the ascendant sits in it. We came across a chart in which the rising sign is Cancer. Its owner Moon is sitting in the eleventh house. The native has been enjoying every kind of benefit from his parents, especially his father. He is already 50 years of age and has hardly any financial problems so far. On the contrary, he owns a big house and property. Thus, this house can be highly beneficial if its owner is beneficially placed but it can also bring bad luck if its owner is placed in the house of waste or expenses, which is the 12th house. Its main concern are friends, contacts, clubs, social groups, humanitarian enterprises, hopes and desires.

The Twelfth House

This house is known as the house of secrets, sorrows and disappointments. It is a 'mystical' house. The famous Western astrologer Steven Forrest calls this house the 'house of troubles' —a point where self meets soul, where ego can merge into spirit. This house can help in leading one to self-transcendence, moving beyond the ego to what is beyond the self.

In fact, it is the house that denotes waste, worthless travel, expenses, and constant worry on account of uncontrolled expenditure, unholy and unwanted errands, bad conduct, losses and unhappiness. If the owner of this house is placed in a good house, such as the 1st, 2nd, 4th, 5th, 7th, 9th, 10th and 11th, it will reduce the benefits of that house. For example, in a native's chart, which has Mars and Saturn in Capricorn in the ascendant, the placement of the owner of the 12th house in the 2nd house will not only make him a spendthrift, but also bring him to the point of bankruptcy.

The natives, in whose chart the owner of the 1st house is placed in the 12th house, will also have problems in some way. It brings a bad name to the native and affects his reputation and public image. Thus, if either the owner of the 12th house is placed in a good house, or the owner of any good house is placed in it, the native is bound to suffer in some way, especially on account of untold expenses. But if its owner is placed in the 6th or 8th house, it may bring some sort of benefit from enemies or help in reducing physical ailments and tensions. Such transits form a kind of yoga known as *Vipreet Rajyoga*. The details will be explained at an appropriate place in the fourth chapter of this book.

Some astrologers hold that this house deals with sacrificial service, repressions, neurosis, hidden enemies, prisons, asylums, occultism, mysticism and secrets.

Characteristics Attributed to the Rising Signs

Details about the rising sun, and how it is placed in an ascendant at the birth of a child, have already been discussed at the beginning of this chapter. Let us now discuss the characteristics of rising signs (symbol) in the ascendant of a native, as it is imperative at this point. But before that there is one important aspect of astrology that we would like to mention for the benefit of the reader. In which sign or symbol is a planet considered to be in its own house(s)? Which are the exalted and debilitated positions of the planets? Without this information, one may not be able to arrive at the correct inferences. The following table unfolds the details of that nature. In order to avoid confusion at this point, we have not mentioned the aspects (look) of the planets on the houses. We shall present it at the appropriate place in the fourth chapter, when a few charts are analysed in some detail.

Table 2:2

Exaltation & Debilitation of Planets in Different Symbols (Houses)

Planet	Own House (Symbol)	Exalted Position	Debilitated Position
Sun	Leo	Aries	Libra
Moon	Cancer	Taurus	Scorpio
Jupiter	Sagittarius, Pisces	Cancer	Capricorn
Mars	Aries, Scorpio	Capricorn	Cancer
Venus	Taurus, Libra	Pisces	Virgo
Mercury	Gemini, Virgo	Virgo	Pisces
Saturn	Capricorn, Aquarius	Libra	Aries

If Aries is rising in the ascendant, it will bestow excellent qualities of character on the native. The native born with this sign will make a considerable impact on others. He will devote great time in completing projects and attaining objectives. Arian (persistent, pursuing) is an element of his personality that will emerge in his/her attitude towards others, while showing kindness and love and in the search for a harmonious and well-balanced life. When this sign rises in the chart, it is largely true that the drive and sense of urgency in life is overwhelmingly powerful in the person. When Mars, the ruler of the sign, also sits in it, the native will enjoy many of these qualities. If the Sun is also in the ascendant, he may enjoy more of these qualities, as it is in its extalted position too. Besides, both the Sun and Mars are permanent friends too, so the results of that nature will be true. But the native who has Aries as the rising sign in the ascendant will also be stubborn, bossy and showy if the Sun and Mars are placed in it.

If Taurus is rising in a chart, the individual will be obsessed with emotional and financial security. The native will have strong ambition and desire to possess beautiful things. The main emphasis in his/her life would be to acquire as much as possible in material terms. The individual will be overconcerned with the amount of money and property he/she owns. There will be less desire and little concern to attain or develop aesthetic values in comparison to material wealth. In emotional relationships, the native will possess a high level of intensity and passion. The native with Taurus rising in the ascendant will be considerably more demanding of his/her partner. The native will be possessive, pleasure-seeking and will also possess a strong element of jealousy, which may often be based on unfounded beliefs and hunches. If Venus is sitting in the ascendant, as it is its own sign, the native will possess such characteristics to a large extent.

If Gemini is rising in the ascendant, it will make the native very talkative. Since Mercury is the owner of this sign, it tends to make the individual very active and good in conversation. He/she will be inclined to be an adventurer. The *jatak* will have singleness of purpose and will always try to keep the objectives of his/her mission in sight. The native will be highly versatile and have a variety of interests. But restlessness will be his/her deep-rooted problem. He/she is restless, which may have a detrimental effect on health. If Mercury is sitting in the ascendant, the native will surely exhibit these characteristics.

If Cancer is rising in the ascendant, it will provide him/her considerable inner strength and determination. The native will have certainty and tenacity of purpose and may even neglect his/her loved ones in attaining objectives and pursuing goals. This is a weakness and the native will do well to remember this and not let it develop into some kind of misunderstanding. With Cancer rising, one of the important characteristics is that the native will be very shrewd, which could be extremely beneficial in business or finance.

But the native may tend to worry too much and also keep problems to himself/herself, which could cause difficulties and health problems. The native's skin is particularly sensitive and such a native may often have a cool and distant attitude towards his/her partner. If the Moon is rising in the ascendant, he/she is likely to enjoy all that to a large extent.

When Leo rises in the ascendant, it will make the individual autocratic. He will be very straightforward, preferring to stick to the truth under any circumstances. The person will grow like a perfectionist but may not be one in the real sense. At times he/she may tend to show off too—a weakness of the sign. But he may be a great administrator and pursue his goals with great care.

When Leo is rising, the person needs to have a partner with a different rising sign or there may be problems. In this case, the best rising signs for the partner would be either Taurus or Pisces, with whom the native may be friends for a long time. It is quite obvious that a native with Leo rising may have a number of problems with romance. He may have a broken heart quite often. Since he/she is extremely dogged in his/her ways in dealing with people, he/she may have problems. Most people may not measure up to the native's expectations, although he/she is very honest and simple as far as his/her own life is concerned. Therefore, for a happy life, the native must learn to be considerate towards others and his/her partner too.

If Virgo is rising, it is likely to develop a strong desire to communicate within the native. A person with Virgo rising in the ascendant will be practical and possess great logic. Due to this affinity for logic, the native needs to develop some sort of self-analysis in order to assess one's actions and disposition towards others objectively.

However, the native with Virgo rising in the ascendant will be a soft and kind-hearted person. He/she will often express tender feelings towards others. It will help the native to develop permanent relationships. When Mercury is rising in Virgo in the ascendant, the native will possess an attractive personality, will express himself/herself very tenderly and enjoy great respect and affection. It is also likely that such a person may not always be truthful, but he/she may do so for the sake of fun. Such a native is likely to take up many tasks at the same time, which prove detrimental to his/her progress. Therefore, one should take great care here. The native should learn to concentrate only on a few things at one time, rather than work many tasks, to avoid failure and disappointments.

When Libra is the rising sign in a chart, one needs to look for a rewarding and permanent relationship with a partner. Although very emotional and affectionate, they show no affection outwardly. Another shortcoming of a Libran is the inability to take quick decisions. A native with Libra in the rising has a natural tendency to be kind-hearted and sympathetic to others. But it does not mean such a person is weak from within.

When Libra is rising in the first house of a native, and is in the ascendant, the seventh house, which is the house related to his/her partner, will naturally bear the sign Aries. As such, he/she has to be very cautious in choosing a life partner because, temperamentally, Libra and Aries are both different in nature. Libra indicates a balance and thus, slow action, while Aries is a fiery, active sign. Thus, amicability in the two is not very common. Libra is prudent in action and mindful in decisions, which are often delayed.

When Scorpio rises in a native's ascendant in a chart (*kundali*), the person is full of energy, drive and dedication. The person's energy resources provide terrific force to his/her mode of expression and life. The majority of such persons' eyes may be very penetrating and the power of force and energy can be seen through them. Such a native will have great power of concentration. He/she will be a demanding partner, full of passion and intensity of feelings. When Scorpio rises, possessiveness towards the partner is quite obvious. For a happy life, this needs to be controlled. If not, it may give birth to jealousy in the other partner. As Scorpio is a fiery sign, the native will be dominating. He/she will often tend to win the argument and like to force his opinions on others. It is not a healthy attitude and needs to be checked, if peace is desired. If Mars is sitting in the ascendant, it is quite likely that the native may choose a profession that may satisfy the inherent, bossy nature. But his/her fury is momentary and settles in seconds, after a sudden burst of emotions.

When Sagittarius rises the native desires to do different kinds of jobs. He/she has a strong tendency to progress in all directions. Like the sign Sagittarius, the native has high aims in life and is ready to take opportunities whenever possible. Generally he/she has a good relationship with the partner. As Jupiter rules Sagittarius and Pisces, both signs can be affected by the placement of a strong Jupiter in the chart.

In case Jupiter is placed in the first house or the ascendant, the native will have a very fine disposition, live like a royal, possess large-heartedness and compassion and cultivate love for the people, especially the downtrodden. His/her relationship with the partner and friends will be very lively. If Jupiter is sitting in the ascendant, as the owner of the first and fourth houses, it will bring prosperity, money, prestige, honour and respect from fellow beings.

Since Sagittarius is a fire sign, it provides great enthusiasm to the native. The *jatak* always likes to express himself/herself in his/her own way and is ready to accept any kind of challenge in life. It may sometimes make one overenthusiastic, leading to problems. But he/she is very positive in outlook, making him/her very spirited and lively.

When Capricorn is rising in a native's chart, he/she will have great stability in life, and common sense that's second to none. As a result, the native is in a position to shape his/her life and plans in an extremely careful and practical way. He/she has a great quality of self-expression and can utilise the potential in an excellent manner. At times, however, one can underestimate oneself, which is not a very healthy quality. Such feelings may occur at times due to lack of confidence or because of the native's inherent shyness.

At times, one may have a great affinity to music and architecture and be inclined towards sculpture. Emotionally the native will be quite tender, sensitive and caring. Once the native is emotionally committed, he/she does so for good.

When Aquarius rises in the ascendant in a chart, the native possesses an inherent need for independence and originality. So the native looks different from others. But he/she is not unpredictable. He/she can be dogmatic and will hardly admit to being wrong. But this person is full of life and tries many interesting, new things. He/she is very kind towards the young and possesses very powerful humanitarian qualities, especially when others need his/her help. He/she can cope with extremely difficult conditions.

Since the person is also often bossy, he/she must try to curtail such feelings. It is imperative for this person to think twice before committing to a permanent relationship, more so as he/she is quite individualistic. Although a private kind of person, the native is also known to be the kindest of all the Zodiac people.

When Pisces is rising in the ascendant of a native's chart, the person possesses both positive and negative qualities. He/she is often kindly disposed but also quite powerfully critical towards others. The native must realise these shortcomings. Like the sign Pisces, which indicates two fish moving in two different directions, the native always looks to the best and the worst sides of life.

This kind of disposition often dampens his/her personality. The native also tends to oppose himself/herself at times, critically examining thoughts and condemning them without much reason. It makes his/her life difficult at times. That is the reason why this person tends to take a different line of action. Yet the native is often emotionally influenced by others, when in difficulty.

When Pisces is rising in the ascendant, people belonging to other signs cannot match the qualities of this person. He/she is prepared to sacrifice anything if it benefits others, and is highly charitable too. At the same time, he/she is also a fault-finder and often tries to look for faults in others. In case Jupiter, the owner of the rising sign, is sitting in the ascendant, it controls two houses—the 1st as well as the 10th—in which the sign Sagittarius is rising. If this is so, the native is likely to enjoy a good reputation at work as he/she is highly agile and active.

Before ending, there are a few other important matters related to understanding astrology properly. Besides the above information, there is a lot about astrology that one has to learn before gaining confidence as an astrologer. The desirous reader needs to be highly objective in his/her approach when reading a horoscope (chart). Without it, one's opinion could be biased and one may be unable to conceive and predict the right results. A regular analysis of the movements of the planets, learning how the *dasha system* operates in predicting matters in the Hindu way of astrology, and the placement of planets in *navmansa**** are a few things that are crucial while learning astrology.

References

A Panchang *is the calendar containing the daily movement of planets, movements of the rising signs and every other necessary information that can help a person learn astrology. It is very handy and extremely popular in India and other countries. It is a ready reckoner that can solve various problems relating to movements of planets, the time of rising of the Sun and the Moon in a particular sign, and the transit of other planets in different signs, etc.*

** *When the Sun enters a new sign in the horizon on a particular date, the rising sign also rises with it for almost two hours on the first day. Thereafter, the rising sign loses approximately four minutes each day. Though it stays in that sign for two hours, its rise starts four minutes before the rise of the Sun on the next day.*

*** Navmansa *is an astrological, scientific procedure which helps to know the strength of a particular planet in a chart. This method has been very popular in the east (India) for a very long time. Every horoscope, cast by a professional astrologer, contains the chart that reflects upon the strength of the planets in view of the* navmansa paddati *(system).*

Chapter Three

The Transit of Planets
(Through Signs and Houses)

The Sun is the centre of the solar system, the source of light, heat and life on earth. It is just like the big boss and is representative of creativity. Therefore, it can affect our actions and achievements to a large extent. The Sun acts like a flashlight. Its track through various Zodiac signs, occupying the 12 houses in a chart, shows which side of a person's personality will be using it most and which areas of life will demand most of the native's (*jatak's*) creative attention. Like the Sun, other planets also track through various signs in the cosmos and affect human lives in different ways. In view of this, since ancient times, through their objective and constant observations, astrologers have identified certain qualities or characteristics that relate to the planets transiting through various Zodiac signs under which people are born.

The nature of a transiting planet describes the types of situations that will arise. Basically, transits represent periods of change. In some way, each transit brings something new that would be interesting to know and to learn the changes that may occur in one's life. Every transit that a person undergoes, adds knowledge and experience to his/her personality and brings something new and different in some form.

Different planets have varying speeds of transit from one sign to another. For example, Jupiter transits from one sign to the other in about a year, the Sun takes one month, the Moon roughly two and a half days, Mars around two and a half months, Mercury about 88 days, and Venus transits the orbit in 225 Earth days, while Saturn takes roughly two and a half years, Pluto roughly 20 years, Neptune completes an orbit of the Sun every 164.79 years, meaning it stays almost 14 years in each sign, while Uranus stays in each sign for seven years. All these transits affect human conduct in totality—their way of life, interests and field of work.

Yearly Journey of the Earth

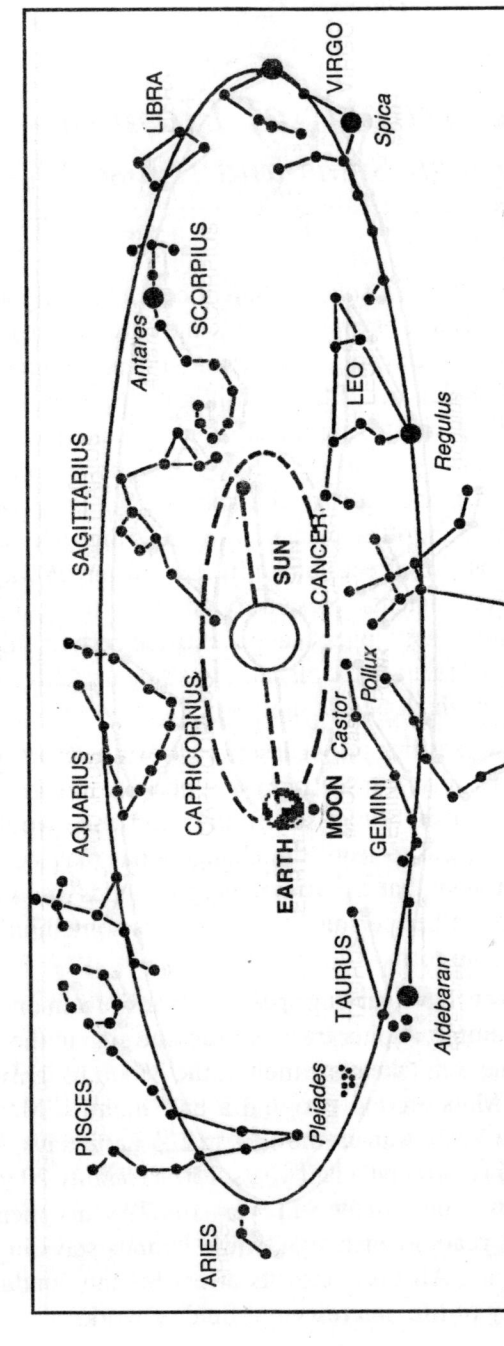

The Earth (whose average distance from the Sun is 93 million miles) revolves around the Sun continuously in elliptical orbit and completes the circuit in 365.25636 days (Sidereal Period) at a speed of 18.51 miles per second or roughly 666000 miles per hour. The mean plane of the Earth's orbit around the Sun is known as *ecliptic*.

The Moon makes one complete circuit of the Earth in 27.3 days (approx.). Average distance of Moon from the Earth is 2.39 lakh miles.

The following pages unfold such characteristics as determined by the Sun and the other planets, tracking from one sign to another. The characteristics of a native born under the Sun, Moon, Mercury, etc. signs may match the description given in this chapter to a large extent. But keeping in view the fact that a native may have been born in cusps, or have some mixed effects created by the impact of various planets placed in the chart at the time of birth, our description of the characteristics may sometimes not tally exactly with all the qualities a native really possesses. Therefore, the reader is requested to keep his/her eyes and mind open and avoid dismal thoughts about astrology if some of his/her qualities don't exactly match our description. It could be caused on account of the impact and aspects (look) of the other planets, besides the Sun, on the individual. As the reader proceeds further in the quest to learn more about astrology, the concepts will gradually become clearer.

Kindly keep in mind that the following description of a person's characteristics under the Sun signs is not exactly the same as in the first chapter of this book. An individual also develops certain other characteristics on account of the impact of the planets transiting in a particular sign and being placed in a particular house in a chart at the time of birth. That's the main theme of this chapter. The effects of these transits and placements are highlighted, with some suitable examples given occasionally. However, more examples along with certain important charts (*kundalis*) are presented in the next chapter for reference.

Let us now examine the transits and placements of each planet separately and see what effects they exert on a native's conduct, career, partner, job opportunities and other aspects. But before proceeding further, **it is also very important to keep in mind which house or houses are controlled (owned) by the transiting planet(s) in a chart.** For example, the native born on 3 March 1962 had Capricorn rising in the ascendant at the time of birth. The owner of Capricorn and Aquarius, Saturn, was sitting in the first house at the time of birth. Therefore, though transiting the first house, Saturn controls both the first and the second houses in the native's chart. Thus, besides the general influence of the Sun, which was in Aquarius at that time, the impact of Saturn and other planets in the chart should also be considered while predicting the native's future. We shall present the full chart of the native born on 3 March 1962 at an appropriate point in the next chapter, and indicate the positions of all the planets in it for reference. It will help in understanding how the strength of each house is determined from the positions and aspects (look) of the transiting planets. Right now, let us discuss the planets rising in a sign and their placements in different houses in a chart and state their influence on individuals.

Transits of the Sun

When the Sun transits through different houses, it may have varied effects on an individual. The Sun represents our vitality and self-expression, so its house positions will show in which sphere of life those energies are likely to be directed by the individual. The Sun, as the most important celestial body for humans, is the most important in a horoscope. Thus, each sign at birth is usually the single most important influence on an individual's personality. As the Sun is associated with life-giving vitality, its placement can be an important indicator of physical vitality. It can also represent important and powerful people in authority. The Sun can also show whether we have a desire for power or an urge to express leadership. The characteristics of the Sun's expression in the signs of the Zodiac are dealt with in the entries on those signs.

When the Sun is in Aries the native tends to be passionate by nature and possesses great enthusiasm for sex. His/her emotions surface quicky. Like the emotional level, the native's physical energy level is very high. Aries is a fire sign so it has enormous warmth, which is endearing to those who are lively and positive in their ways and manner. The body area of Aries is the head. The native may suffer from headaches.

When the Sun transits in the first house (ascendant) of a native's chart, it inspires a person to express physically. Self-absorption may be the result of the emphasis on the first house. He/she may tend to show off, even where clothes are concerned. The native is mostly uncomplicated in his/her attitude to life. The person plans everything in a straightforward manner. The basic motivation is to push ahead and not lag behind opportunities. Such a person has a lot of determination but needs to cultivate patience, since this is lacking. The individual must also be aware of tendencies like selfishness and try to counter them as much as possible.

When the Sun is in Taurus it may help the native making good money in life. He or she will tend to lead a very happy life. All that the native earns is through his/her own ability. A Taurus person will do well in banking and multinational companies. His/her body area is the throat, which is often prone to colds, sore throat and loss of voice. As the ruling planet is Venus, he/she is a good-looking person, loves rich food and is fond of sweets. The native tends to put on weight, which he/she must try to control to live a healthy life. The person is mostly a loving parent. He/she loves music, which often becomes an important form of self-expression. Some natives love embroidery, sewing, pottery and sculpture too. Basically the native possesses artistic tastes. This is the best pursuit for the native in life.

When the Sun transits the second house of a native's chart, his/her outstanding virtue is generosity. The native knows through experience that there are no shortcuts in life. He/she has patience to listen to others and tends to do different things in life. The native is very fond of living in well-furnished and decorative homes and loves to own beautiful things. The native prefers to work hard to achieve ever-increasing materialistic needs.

If the Sun is in Gemini in the native's chart he/she will possess great versatility. Such individuals are never interested in one area of work and like to pursue different things. The ruling planet of this sign, Mercury, gives the native the power and quality of communication. As such, he/she will contribute to newspapers, radio, or television. He/she will tend to be somewhat brooding towards the partner. The native also tends to be in a hurry all the time, which is evident by the person's fast gait.

Basically, a Geminian is quite rational and logical but his/her worst fault is superficiality, which needs to be mitigated by developing proper understanding. A Geminian can make a successful career in the media, as an interviewer, or in telecommunications. The native will be good at debates and discussions. So, being a lawyer would also suit the person. He/she can work as a superb salesperson, and excel in advertising as well. The native will tend to keep a youthful appearance and be highly mobile. The body areas of the native are the shoulders, arms, hands and lungs. To live happily, he/she must keep away from tension and restlessness.

When the Sun transits the third house in a native's chart, the most dominant characteristic of the individual is his/her intellect. Even if the native feels that something has been lacking in his/her early education, he/she will have this great urge and desire to make up for it. Having achieved that, the native would like to go even further.

When the Sun is rising in Cancer the native is extremely tenacious and hardworking. Once the individual decides to take action, there's no turning back. The native possesses great powers of intuition and, therefore, his/her chances of being right are very high. But the native is quite prone to worry. To stop this tendency, the Cancer person must follow his/her instincts. The native is highly charged emotionally, which is also not very healthy. Such natives do well in the hotel line, catering, navy, teaching, as antique dealers or historians. The native is also a great parent, a sensuous lover, possesses a natural tendency to say harsh things and gets upset when criticised. The native's body area is the chest. It is quite likely that his/her digestive system may go bad on account of excess worry.

When the Sun transits the fourth house in a native's chart, his/her vitality and self-expression will find a positive outlet in building a good home and happy family. The native will possess a basic instinct to protect loved ones. An element of creative energy will be channelled through the individual, who may develop interests such as decoration, sewing and other work that enhances the beauty of the home.

When the Sun is in Leo the individual likes to live in his/her own kingdom. The native possesses a great ability to lead and, therefore, tends to interfere in others' lives as well, in order to organise it for them. The native is quick to help others improve. He/she will be a spendthrift, possess creative potential and will be ambitious too. Though the native is magnanimous, he may be accused of bossiness. A Leo believes that life is for living and enjoying to the fullest. He/she will work hard to fulfil this ambition. Enthusiasm and a positive fiery emotion are very much part of the person's character. The positive side of a Leo's personality is to put all efforts for continued personal development. He/she is always a caring parent, who regularly encourages the children to grow, whether in school or in their private lives. A Leo's body area is the back and so, he/she may suffer from back pains. The native generally possesses a straight back and walks well.

When the Sun transits the fifth house in a native's chart, it shines very brightly as it is in its own house, Leo. The native will be highly ambitious. Creativity and an urge to express it will mostly be present in the individual. The native should ensure that this creative urge actually finds an expression and does not remain a mere tool for showing off. As it is the house of children, the native is advised not to push children too hard into his or her way of thinking. Let them have their own way as far as possible.

When the Sun is in Virgo the individual is surrounded with many great tasks. Although not blessed with as much organisational ability as persons born under other Zodiac signs, the native does not like to relax. Such a person is very logical and enormously practical. But, at times, he/she may get involved with things that may cause tension. It may also have a negative effect on one's digestion. However, the native likes to be involved in many things and develops various hobbies to fill the time fruitfully. A person born with Virgo as the Sun sign is always very popular, as he/she is willing to help others. A Virgoan deals so resolutely from within that often he/she does not like to listen to others. The native is very modest in love and a caring partner too. Many Virgoans love to cultivate vegetarianism and tend to enjoy food. It may result in obesity at times. A Virgoan is quite a gifted analyst. His/her talents lie in areas requiring research and a systematic approach. The native likes to act quickly but does not like it if his/her decisions are ill considered.

When the Sun is placed in the sixth house of a native's chart it may provide a sense of duty and emphasise routine. Since the Sun is in the sixth house, the house of Mercury, the native may tend to develop creative writing ability and cultivate the art of communication as well. Such an individual will find great satisfaction in most fields of work aligned to communication. Being of service to others and working as a personal assistant may also be a source of satisfaction to the individual.

When the Sun is in Libra such a native tends to keep a balance in his/her emotions and activities. A Libran is not a loner and has a great deal of love for his/her lover. The native loves peaceful existence. When it comes to decisions, he/she prefers to wait before committing anything. Such a person does not like to rush but is not always late. He/she has excellent negotiating abilities. During spare time he/she may like to be an interior designer and may be inclined to tasks relating to beauty and music. The native can also make an excellent accompanist and dressmaker, loves social dances and may even love playing tennis. Libra rules the kidneys and the Libran may suffer kidney ailments.

When the Sun transits the seventh house of a native's chart, there is a great possibility that the person with this sort of Sun placement may be totally committed to the partner. Much is likely to be given to the partner physically and emotionally, as the Sun will like to express itself in this manner. Therefore, the native is advised to keep a balance in his/her emotional activities lest he/she become too docile due to their great attachment. Reliance on the partner must not be so great that, during low points in the relationship, it creates psychological problems for the native.

When the Sun is in Scorpio in a native's chart, it provides abundant emotional and physical energy. A person having the Sun in Scorpio is capable of a lot. The more he/she does, the better the individual feels. But when the abundant resources stagnate, the native is at his/her worst. The native gets bored if his/her talents are wasted. He/she possesses great emotional intensity. The element of sex is sometimes overstretched in the person. It is also largely true that the person sometimes becomes obsessed with drive and determination. He/she is a natural detective of the Zodiac. He/she can make a great researcher, a scientist, and an engineer and can also hold prominent positions in the armed forces. He may be especially attracted towards wine and the oil trade. The native often enjoys demanding sports, such as boxing, and also likes the arts in general, and driving, underwater sports and swimming are often rewarding for him. The native's body areas are the genitals and he can be vulnerable to throat infections.

When the Sun transits the eighth house in a native's chart, it may develop great emotional intensity and purposeful force in the individual. The native may tend to be highly introspective, which is not very healthy. The driving force of the Sun for an individual may develop in the direction of sex but for others it may lead the individual to amass wealth. Such an individual may have a tendency to live in the hope of good inheritance, especially when Neptune opposes the Sun in the chart.

When the Sun is in Sagittarius one feels a strong desire to express oneself. Undemanding work cannot make the individual happy. As it is a fire sign, it provides the individual high levels of enthusiasm for life and his interests. He/she is keen to enjoy all aspects of life in a very positive way and is very versatile. He/she loves sports and tends to take to physical exercises. The native is philosophically oriented and is often restless to know every side of life. Restlessness, in fact, is one of the major faults of the native. If the native can sort out his/her real objectives, this can easily be mended. A Sagittarius can be crude, a wild wanderer, mostly seeking adventure, and freedom from all restraint. At times, such a person can be reckless and excessively blunt, and sometimes irresponsible too. But the native is certainly quite humorous, entertaining and optimistic. The individual likes wisdom and makes a very inspiring teacher. The native constantly aspires to higher wisdom and greater spiritual insight.

When the Sun transits the ninth house in a chart, it will direct the individual to cultivate intellectual growth and broaden his/her mind and body horizons. Tending to live in a world of dreams, such natives are advised to be more practical to become productive, for dreams are not the real state of growth and achievement. With this placement of the Sun, the native has the potential to achieve a great deal in terms of physical and mental growth. In terms of career, the scope is quite wide. He/she may be interested in publishing, and may do well in higher education. As he/she possesses a flair for languages, there may be opportunities for assignments abroad. But the native's great need is the freedom of expression. He/she possesses a great sense of fun and always likes to live in roomy, windowed rooms. The native also loves hunting. He gets bored with a partner who does not have a sense of fun. His/her physical problem is putting on weight, which requires to be checked.

75

When the Sun is in Capricorn the individual, like its sign the Goat, is surefooted. He/she works doggedly, negating difficulties and negotiating problems carefully. The native is determined to reach the top and follows a carefully charted path. Every decision he/she takes is considered carefully, and every challenge and opportunity is assessed properly so that risks are minimal. This is the quality he shares with the mountain goat, climbing very carefully but doggedly. The other half of the Capricorn sign is the fishtail, which indicates a poor, domestic kind of animal that has no desire to reach the top. So, at times, a negative, hopeless attitude makes its presence felt in the individual. But it has been observed that from time to time the individual tends to reverse his/her role.

The native also possesses a great, offbeat sense of humour. A serious-minded Capricornian will suddenly come up with a witty remark. The native does not show too many emotions. Such an individual possesses a tendency of being cool in love. But once committed, the native displays considerable amount of loyalty towards his loved one. The native will often have a considerable sense of pride. An inherent ambition inspires the individual to aspire to move up the social ladder. The individual will often have a desire to impress other people. The body areas of the native are knees and shins, teeth, skin and bones. His/her bones are often vulnerable. He/she is a demanding parent and needs to develop warmth and sensibility.

When the Sun transits the tenth house, it confers great vitality on the individual and may help him/her achieve worldly power of some kind. From many points of views, it is a very powerful placement of the Sun, which could bring success in a political career or any other sort of career. If the individual can avoid cultivating autocratic tendencies that are quite likely to grow in him/her on account of the Sun in the tenth house, the native could be a great achiever in life. If the Sun is in Capricorn, there is a great possibility that the native will be very practical and his/her intellectual abilities will be at their peak. But much depends on the placement of Saturn, which should not be in opposition to the Sun to lessen its good effects on the individual.

When the Sun is in Aquarius in the chart of an individual, he/she grows as a most individualistic type of person. The native is one of the kindest, most helpful and friendly persons in the Zodiac. Because of the nature of the sign, the native is an extremely private person and does not like to get emotionally involved with other people. The native has great originality and a real flair for life, which can be used in a variety of fields if allowed full expression. Such a native often does well in glamorous professions, like theatre, television, beauty or any other area where the individual can express his/her originality freely. Many such individuals are very successful in the field of science, archaeology and geology.

Such a person is often a forward-looking parent. But he/she must learn to respect the children's needs to make them grow free and better. The body areas of the native are the ankles. It is, therefore, very necessary to keep them moving to stay fit. The native mostly likes skiing, good extensive exercise, dance, acrobatics and athletics as well.

When the Sun transits the eleventh house in a chart, it inspires the individual to make his/her mark within the community he/she lives in. Very often the native will be involved in humanitarian activities and indulge in charitable and fund-raising tasks for the benefit of the community. But such tasks may tend to keep them away from their families. If the native desires to lead a happy life, this must be avoided. Social life could be good, but too much of it may be troublesome, especially for the near and dear ones.

When the Sun is in Pisces in a chart, the individual may tend to be a poet. The native's eyes reveal that he/she is very emotional. The native possesses a tendency to oppose himself like the sign Pisces, which contains two fish facing opposite directions. Such an individual takes a totally different line of action. He/she is the kindest and most charitable of all the signs. The native tends to make many sacrifices for others. It is a trait that he/she shares with the opposite sign. At times, the individual also has monk or priest-like aspirations. The individual can do very well in medical and caring professions. With a great desire to be a poet, a Piscean may aspire to write in verse. The native can make a good dancer, be involved in the fine arts and make a warm lover. His/her body area is the feet. The tendency to worry may lead to stomach problems.

When the Sun transits the twelfth house in a chart, it may lead to withdrawal tendencies in an individual. The native may be an introvert and lack self-confidence. Being the house related to waste and expenditure, the Sun may bring desperate tendencies in the individual. He/she may be a spendthrift and waste both time and money on unproductive work and habits. The individual must guard against such tendencies.

Transits of the Moon

Like the Sun, the Moon also exerts tremendous influence on a native, but the areas it tends to influence most are human emotions, moods and temporary behaviour. It has been observed that when the Moon is full in the orbit, such influences are tremendously high. Observations have revealed that when there is a full moon in the sky, some people become emotionally unbalanced. When graduating from an established college situated in Agra, the city of the Taj Mahal, we happened to visit a mental hospital on a full Moon day. To our great surprise, we found that although patients were on medication for months and had shown great improvement in their condition, many had suddenly lost their mental balance on that day.

In fact, the Moon's influence on a native should be very fruitful if its placement is beneficial in a native's chart. It can influence one's personality in many ways and provide him/her with wealth, knowledge, good finances, sharp reflections, spirit of cooperation and attitude of adaptability, besides influencing moods and emotions.

Let us examine what influence the Moon signs bestow on human characteristics, when it transits from one sign to the other.

When the Moon is in Aries in an individual's chart it inspires instinctive actions and reactions in most situations. That means the individual tends to act on the spur of the moment in reaction to a situation. This usually causes problems. Such a person needs to exercise restraint and learn from experience when to react and when not to do so. Such people are also capable of inspiring actions in others, as the sign the Moon transits is fiery, impulsive, wrathful, warm and ambitious.

When the Moon is transiting through the first house of a native's chart, it will have a very strong influence on the individual, if it is within 8 to 10 degrees of the ascending sign. In that case, it will have a great effect on the native's personality, with reference to his/her reactions, responses and care for loved ones. If the placement of the Moon is strong when it is nearer in degrees from the sign rising at the ascendant, the individual may also be self-expressive.

When the Moon is in Taurus it is a positive sign of the Moon, which enjoys an exalted position in this sign. The native tends to take calculated risks when the Moon is in Taurus in his/her chart. He/she will also be quite prudent and be able to take care of his/her problems carefully and quite successfully. Such a person will be less emotional and more practical. He/she will also possess great determination and have excellent communication skills. A Taurean is quite clever and able to comprehend and deal with difficult problems effectively. Since the native is farsighted, he/she is not stubborn and less emotional. But though prudent, he/she is likely to suffer from overconfidence, which stems from the belief that he/she knows everything.

When the Moon transits the second house in a native's chart it makes the individual achieve a strong sense of personal security, both emotional and financial. There is a strong instinct to save, as it adds to the native's sense of security. The natives must protect themselves against feelings of obsession, which could lead them to woe rather than happiness. It may also make the individual selfish.

When the Moon is in Gemini the native's reactions to situations will be remarkably quick. The person will possess a keen sense of awareness. He/she may be very witty and provide discreet answers to questions put to him/her. These answers stem from deep-rooted intuition. But restlessness and a strong desire for change might become the native's problem. Such a person may lack deep concentration and interest in other people. As a positive effect of the Moon in Gemini, the native will make a positive contribution in various fields and use logic as his/her tool for it.

When the Moon transits the third house in a native's chart, the need to communicate is supreme. Such an individual should move around to meet people and to satisfy the need. The native will have an instinctive need for education but this is not real. He/she needs to convert that superficial feeling into a real one if he/she wants any benefits from the Moon's placement in the third house. The Moon in this house bestows good imagination. Such persons are loved by their children because they are able to use this talent to churn out exciting bedtime stories. The placement of the Moon in this house may develop a sense of cunningness and cleverness in the native, especially when he/she is challenged in arguments.

When the Moon is in Cancer it is its own sign. It has a very powerful bearing on the native's emotions and makes him/her prudent. It also positively affects the native's instincts and intuitions. Basically a good sign, it helps the individual retain balance of mind when surrounded by difficult circumstances. There cannot be a better example than presenting the reader Sri Rama's chart (*kundali*), in which the Moon in Cancer is rising in the ascendant. Most of us know about Sri Rama's qualities and, also, how balanced He was even when surrounded by most difficult circumstances. Such a person is highly tolerant, logical, and very realistic. Although emotional, the person is well balanced in emotions too. If female, such a person makes for a caring mother too.

When the Moon transits the fourth house of a native's chart it creates a great urge and need for a home and family. Its good placement, say in Cancer or in any friendly sign, may develop a good sense of security for the family. It may help the native build a comfortable house for the family. At the same time, it may create an introverted tendency on account of the native's caring and protective attitude.

When the Moon is in Leo it tends to influence the native to be a good inspiration to others. The native has a deep desire to reach the top when the Moon rises in Leo. It also leads to a tendency in the native to be autocratic and dogmatic. The individual needs to control this tendency. The Moon in Leo is often likely to give a wrong impression about the individual, although he tries hard to ratify it. Being the owner of the twelfth house, when it rises in Leo at the ascendant in a chart, it tends to make the native a miser. Besides, it often tempts the individual not to tell the truth when required.

When the Moon transits the fifth house in a chart it tends to develop creative ability in the native. This urge, however, can also be directed towards rearing children in the best possible manner. Doing the right thing for children comes instinctively to the native. This is also the house of lovemaking. If the placement of the Moon is good, the native will indulge in love from a purely

80

procreative aspect rather than mere indulgence for pleasure. At times the individual may be showy and talkative. This is likely to happen when the Moon is placed in a bad sign, or is weak in degrees when transiting in a sign at the time of the birth of an individual.

When the Moon is rising in Virgo it makes the individual very practical, helpful and extremely logical. The individual always tends to crosscheck information before accepting it. Since such an individual often helps others, he may be very successful in the medical profession or with any other social organisation. Such an individual is mostly down-to-earth, sensible and highly reliable. He/she has great literary tastes and jobs related to writing could bring the native great success in life. Such a native is often extravagant and likes to lead a luxurious life.

When the Moon transits in the sixth house in a chart, this placement of the planet exerts an important effect on the health and well-being of the native. The Moon's influence on the health of the individual will be great if it is placed within ten degrees in its rising sign. Placed in the seventh house, it is automatically in opposition to the ascendant. Depending on its strong and weak placement in the seventh house, and according to its rising sign in the chart, it may create good and bad effects on the individual. It is very important that the native develops good and steady habits and overcomes negative habits like smoking, drinking or taking drugs. If the Moon is in Taurus in the seventh house and has its full aspect at the ascendant, the native must be extremely careful regarding these habits.

The Moon rises in Libra in the chart of an individual, making the native think twice before taking any action. There is no sudden rushing into things. Often the native possesses a calm appearance, is usually good and balanced in crises, and doesn't panic easily. When the Moon is in Libra, there is an element of bravery mixed with kindness and sympathy for the needy. Since the Balance is the sign that the Moon is occupying, the native is also quite balanced in his/her conduct and can act as an excellent mediator between two opposing sides.

When the Moon is transiting the seventh house in a native's chart, it makes him/her able to respond well and sensibly to the partner's needs if it is powerful and is in a good or friendly sign. At times, this lunar influence over moods can cause problems. Sometimes emotions are provoked just to attract the partner's attention and increase the warmth of his/her affection. But such outbursts can be damaging. The native must keep this in mind.

When the Moon rises in Scorpio it tends to cause an imprudent outburst of the individual's powerful emotions. However, the native has the quality to inspire others. Jealousy is one of the native's big drawbacks. Therefore, the native should try to keep a check on his/her emotions, which are likely to spring forth and hurt someone, especially in difficult circumstances. The Moon is in its lowest ebb as far as this sign is concerned. So, the individual must exert great force to control emotions and develop the inner strength that he often lacks.

When the Moon is transiting the eighth house in a native's chart, the instinctive Moon is in a house where intuition, emotion and deep-rooted feelings are emphasised. If a powerful moon is in this house, some individuals may also possess a sixth sense. By 'powerful' we mean rising from 10 to 22 degrees in the sign in the eighth house and also be in a friendly sign. The native will have a strong sexual instinct, which may demand frequent expression. The native's emotional resources are considerably great, but jealousy and suspicion are also likely to grow in the native if the Moon is well placed in this house.

The Moon in Sagittarius will bestow good influences on the individual, as it is in its most friendly sign. The native will have a tendency to respond to all the situations in a quick and enthusiastic manner. His/her disposition and exhibition of emotions, even in an offhand manner, will be quite balanced and prudent. Therefore, the native will often be respected for his/her opinions. But such a native will also possess a desire to express his/her views freely, which may need to be curtailed at times. The Moon in this sign often makes a person quite ambitious, which can be good if efforts to achieve goals are followed prudently. The native needs to check impulsiveness, which can sometimes put him/her in difficult situations. The native possesses a great urge to move forward, and traffic jams add to his/her impatience. The native can sometimes give the impression of knowing much more than is really the case. Hope and feelings of optimism run very high in the individual. Such unrealistic feelings need to be curtailed. To have hope is not bad but to possess it unrealistically is a recipe for disaster.

When the Moon transits the ninth house in a chart, the native will possess a great desire to fulfil instinctive needs through studies. On account of weak concentration, however, he/she may not have the desired success. If a strong Moon is not assisted by the good placement of Jupiter in the chart, the native's goals may not be fulfilled. The native may possess too many emotions, which will often not allow him/her to reach goals. Therefore, the individual must keep his/her feet on the ground rather indulge in fantasies or drift away with emotions. As already stated before, besides luck, this house denotes travel and the individual may be inclined to travel. His/her intellect is philosophical but takes moral decisions quite instinctively. But the native mostly tends to find truth that leans towards more practice and less imagination.

When the Moon rises in Capricorn the native often tends to react to situations. He/she likes to meet people in a cool and calm manner, to the extent of exhibiting aloofness in conduct. The native has a tendency to grumble about things that go wrong. The individual is often very ambitious and needs to try hard to overcome his/her lack of confidence. Such a native may possess a great desire to reach colossal heights in life but will have to learn to be pragmatic to reach such positions.

When the Moon is transiting the tenth house in a native's chart, it indicates that the individual may have the potential for fame in some field, especially in his/her chosen one. People over whom the individual has some authority are likely to respect and love him/her most. The flow of the native's institutional power will be quite extensive for those whom he/she thinks his/her care is required. If the Moon is in Capricorn, the native will show his emotional care quite coolly. If it is in Leo, the care will be shown quite dogmatically. The native will often desire change and variety in his/her career. Even if he/she becomes famous, he/she may still have a variety of accomplishments.

When the Moon rises in Aquarius in a native's chart, it shines with clear brilliance. The native has real glamour and dynamic power of attraction. The native possesses much kindness and a deep desire to help those in need of it. He/she will be greatly moved by human suffering. At times, while speaking, the native may offer unexpected responses. Sometimes, when the Moon is rising in Aquarius in a native's chart, individuals may show lack of warmth, passion and expression of true feelings. When the Moon is in Aquarius, Saturn governs this sign. It may affect the individual with negative feelings and make him/her suffer loneliness and depression.

If the Moon transits the eleventh house in a chart, the individual may tend to lead a great social life and always like to be part of a group. However, this can cause damage to the individual's independent needs and freedom. Therefore, the native must analyse his real reasons for sticking to a group. If not, the individual may lose a part of his/her sense of identity. The influence of the sign is often so potent on the individual that he/she is usually introverted. Getting close to him/her is generally not so easy.

When the Moon rises in Pisces it tends to leave a great effect on the individual's emotions and intuition. Both the characteristics may often surface in the native, especially when someone wants his/her help. Such a person may be inclined to deception and may dislike insignificant circumstances. Such reactions may lead him/her to endless confusion. The native usually has no patience for constructive work and, therefore, needs to reorganise himself/herself in a truly positive way. In fact, this placement of the Moon shows that the individual possesses two kinds of forces that are highly charged. When the Moon falls in this sign, the emotional content of Pisces is very powerful. Easily moved, his/her responses to all situations is highly emotional. It is quite likely that, under difficult circumstances, the native may turn out to be weak and unable to face them.

When the Moon transits the twelfth house in a chart, it will bestow considerable sense of kindness and emotional warmth on the individual. If a strong Moon is placed in the house, the emotional warmth will still be strong. The native will have a strong urge to make sacrifices. But it will depend on a strong placement of the Moon in the chart. At the same time, the native may also possess a tendency to deceive people and a negative attitude of escapism.

84

The native will often not like to discuss his/her problems with loved ones. At times the individual may show withdrawal tendencies and at another time he may be quite vocal. He/she may also show signs of being highly spiritual and also love rock music. This is perhaps on account of the nature of the sign, Pisces.

Transits of Mercury

Mercury, one of the swift-moving ancient gods of Greece, has more positive aspects to bestow upon its natives. A progressive placement of Mercury helps the individual greatly in decision-making. When placed in the ascendant, it provides the individual fairly good looks and makes him/her quite attractive to others. It bestows upon the native the quality of conversation and swiftness in character, which is not very common with people of other Zodiac signs. Mercury's main area of influence is the mind, particularly the part that relates with perception, reason and communication. Usually this planet does not stay far away from the Sun. So it has a special relationship with the Sun and is never further than 28 degrees from it. Therefore, we align our description of Mercury's characteristics mostly to the Sun, although it also has certain distinct qualities of its own. Mercury is associated with travel and communication. The Romans considered Mercury as the god of commerce and trade, so its association with travel and communication is quite natural. Mercury is also associated with writing and teaching.

When Mercury is in Aries it almost acts like its sign and makes the native very impulsive. In this way it affects his/her mental make-up. Quick decisions are good but imply impulsiveness as well. This also means lack of patience with decisions and needs to be checked by the native. But this tendency also leads to a positive outlook and provides the individual with greater confidence and self-assurance. These individuals are blessed with the ability to take the initiative. They also love debating and arguing.

When Mercury transits the first house in a chart, its influence will be very powerful. It will provide the native a bright personality. The native's need to communicate will be very strong. He/she will be very quick in action and greatly talkative. Quite often, the native will possess a generous disposition. If Mercury is well placed in this house or if the house has its aspects, it will add colour to the

85

native's outlook and personality. Good aspects or placements will make the native optimistic and bad aspects may lead him/her to pessimism. If Mercury is nearer to the ascendant in degrees, it is likely to influence the native more—often in a positive manner.

When Mercury is in Taurus in the chart of an individual, it causes him/her to think very carefully and constructively. The native is always cautious and plans quite constructively in a methodical and disciplined manner. When Mercury is rising in Taurus in the chart, the individual is more or less very practical. This sort of placement aids an individual's memory, and also affects his/her conduct, leading to stubbornness. Being in its friendly sign, Mercury affects the thinking abilities of the individual. It makes him/her slow, steady, deliberate and very careful about what he/she says to others.

When Mercury transits the second house in a chart, it encourages a quick and clever attitude towards money. The native will have a strong desire to become rich overnight. But how much that desire can be fulfilled will depend largely on Mercury's good or bad placement in the chart. Positive aspects from Saturn will help the individual get what he/she desires, but negative aspects from Neptune could lead to confusion, deceit and even fraud. The native's bargaining ability will be good. The native is likely to enjoy two or more sources of income.

When Mercury is in Gemini the native will tend to think quickly. He/she will possess a certain kind of brightness, which is not common to people of the other signs. It will help the native through difficult situations. The native's ability to take quick decisions is a great help during difficult times. At the same time the native will be extremely talkative. It means the individual will be good at communication.

The individual may do a lot of travelling, which he/she loves. This sign will provide the individual a more rational outlook. The native will also be less emotional. The talents of the native lie in his/her ability to communicate. Such an individual possesses quick wit and is able to see all aspects of a situation very clearly. However, the individual's mental make-up is such that he/she tends to blame others for what he/she does wrong.

When Mercury transits the third house in a chart, it will create great curiosity in the native. His/her needs to communicate will be accelerated immensely. The native will like to spend more time in writing, and expressing his/her thoughts in some form or way. Such a native will possess great mental ability and powers of perception. He will be mentally and intellectually very alert and possess an inquisitive mind. Although the native possesses a quest for knowledge, at times this may be at a superficial level only. The native will have a lot of skill in communication at work. Such natives possess great potential for a career in the media and jobs associated with publishing and printing.

When Mercury is in Cancer the native possesses superb memory. He/she is somewhat sentimental but extremely imaginative. However, there is also a tendency to look to the past. It affects forward thinking and planning and causes apprehensions and worry because of the fear of the unknown. But such individuals can be great historians. The native can also be an excellent storywriter for children. If Mercury rises in Cancer, it may affect logical thinking and lead to worry.

When Mercury transits the fourth house of a native's chart, it will make him think more of home and family. He/she will spend much of his/her time in thinking often about them. The individual will possess a constant need to shift residence. It may be caused on account of some kind of inner conflict in the native. It has been observed that mothers may have a significant influence on such individuals.

When Mercury is in Leo in a chart, it provides the native with excellent planning ability. Such a native will always like to work in an orderly and sensible way. But he/she can be dogmatic in approach and quite stubborn. The native will be expressive in a pompous and old-fashioned way, with a tendency to show off. However, he/she will come up with great ideas at times, and will be greatly determined and practical. The native will be highly enthusiastic, possess great mental energy, and have good power of concentration, especially when studying. His/her speech can be quite dramatic.

When Mercury transits the fifth house in a chart, it may influence the native to take more risks and create some kind of gambling instinct in him. Being the house of love, Mercury will create an ability to communicate to his/her mate in a very affectionate manner. The individual will be attracted to leisurely pursuits that challenge the intellect. Well-placed Mercury will endow the native with a lot of patience and help him/her reach defined objectives.

When Mercury is in Virgo in a native's chart, it often tends to keep him/her in a lively mood. It also tends to make the individual most practical and constructive. In fact, it is the second sign that Mercury rules and also occupies it in exaltation. It endows the individual with many humane qualities and material benefits. The native will be highly interested in intellectual work and have the confidence to develop most of his/her abilities.

The native will also possess great nervous energy and often be fully immersed in work. Since such an individual will have great common sense and practical ability, these qualities will help him/her do his/her best in life. Not only will the native think practically and constructively, he/she will be able to cope with demanding intellectual work. The native is likely to possess highly charged nervous energy, which needs to be expended to keep the stomach in order or even to save oneself from migraines.

When Mercury transits the sixth house in a chart, its influence on the native is quite strong as it is its own Virgo house. The native is inclined to vegetarianism. As he/she is fond of good food, it may lead to weight and stomach problems. It can also tend to create a liking for routine and for serving others. The native will be an able communicator, with an ability to accept things after a critical analysis and evaluation.

When Mercury is in Libra it tends to increase sympathy, kindness and great consideration for others in the native. But the native is also likely to develop indecisiveness. It is observed that the individual becomes slow in concentration and is unable to keep focus. He/she slows down where oral or other modes of expression are concerned. The individual tends to keep away from controversial subjects and situations. But he/she possesses a romantic outlook towards life and has a tendency to be overoptimistic. The individual is often relaxed with other people and can develop satisfactory emotional relationships.

When Mercury rises in the seventh house in a chart, it is possible the native may be influenced into his/her partner's way of thinking. This may not be good in the long run, as he/she may lose the freedom to take decisions. But it is a good house as far as business partnership is concerned. A strong placement of Mercury may help the individual be a good lawyer. The native can also act as a great mediator and negotiate well.

When Mercury is in Scorpio it provides the individual great intensity and intuitive powers. This intensified intuition is often combined with logical and rational approach, induced with the curiosity to know more. He/she will develop a deep desire to find out facts and to know the precise reasons for things. The native is likely to possess a great longing to solve problems and to get down to the most minute details of any aspect of life. He/she will have real potential for a career as a researcher, analyst or psychologist. The native will possess great powers of observation and communication. The individual may also possess a great sense of purpose and determination, and a fascination for mysteries and occult.

When Mercury transits the eighth house in a chart, the native may possess psychic abilities and like to indulge in thinking about matters related to life and death. An above-average preoccupation with sexuality is often present. The native will possess an inquisitive and searching mind. He/she may be a good researcher and may be involved in studies relating to mystery areas. The native will possess intuitive powers and rational enthusiasm to tackle problems.

When Mercury is in Sagittarius in a chart, it causes an individual to devote time to compelling interests. He/she possesses versatility and a natural flair for language. The native's outlook becomes enormously optimistic and tolerant towards others' stuffy attitude. The native also possesses a great vision to instantly grasp even the most complicated plans or ideas. But the native may also be restless and superficial in many matters. Such acts need to be checked.

When Mercury transits the ninth house in a native's chart, if placed positively, it obviously influences the native's intellect. The native will love travelling and dream of journeys abroad. Constant planning may find his dreams coming to fruition. Quite often the native may choose a career that offers the opportunity to travel. The individual may possess a craving for intellectual work. Consequently, he/she may enjoy working in libraries, bookstores and universities.

When Mercury is in Capricorn it provides a cool and clever temperament and keeps the native's moods steady. It enlightens the native on how to evaluate all situations in a clever and careful way. Such a native will have a flair for mathematics. In fact, the native possesses a fertile mind and enjoys solving problems he/she encounters. The native's entire approach to life is quite serious. The sign Capricorn provides the native great thoughts that help him/her progress and achieve objectives. But the native tends to underestimate all his/her achievements.

When Mercury transits the tenth house, it is quite likely that the native will have many changes of career. As it is a natural house of Saturn, Mercury's rising in a friendly sign like Capricorn, Taurus or Virgo can bestow benefits from changing jobs. In such friendly signs, Mercury will make the person more responsible towards himself and others. With high responsibility, the individual will also possess mobility with which he/she will be able to achieve life's goals. The native must guard against boredom caused by lack of work. It may weaken his peace of mind and cause restlessness.

When Mercury is in Aquarius it gives the individual originality and a quick mind. It can also add an element of stubbornness and a slight leaning towards eccentricity, mixed with some sort of brilliance. The native possesses the potential to follow a different line of thought when dealing with difficult problems. With persistent efforts the individual develops various talents that help him/her tackle unusual circumstances in life. The native possesses plenty of bright ideas and a great ability to communicate in a friendly manner with all kinds of people. Originality and independence of outlook and a great aptitude to rationalise things help the individual take a detached view of every situation in life.

When Mercury transits in the eleventh house in a chart, the native will possess a great desire to have many friends and have an impelling need to communicate. The individual may have a deep desire to participate in community and social work, which the person will find fulfilling. In fact, deep and meaningful friendship may have little meaning for the native, who is more fascinated with social relationships.

When Mercury is in Pisces the individual is often seen in a great mood. The native is mostly kind and considerate to people and ready to help them. He/she is very pleasant, gentle and often displays a high level of emotion towards the family and others. But he/she is not very practical. The native is often very forgetful, creating problems for himself/herself. At times, the individual may try and conceal this habit. The native may also be interested in the occult.

When Mercury transits the twelfth house in a native's chart, it can lead to conflict between logic, intuition as well as the emotions of the individual. The native may tend to waste time in talking a lot on phones and to people from whom he/she may not benefit. So the native is advised to rationalise emotions and use intuition with prudence. Such natives may possess love for literature, especially poetry. They can do well with media or communications related to technology or engineering.

Transits of Venus

The Planet Venus, one of the ancient Greek gods symbolising beauty and love, is considered to be highly beneficial in the astrological world. It rules Taurus and Libra among the Zodiac signs and people born under these Sun signs tend to possess the characteristics they govern. Under the influence of Venus, the native will possess the qualities of love and appreciation of beauty. He/she will avoid ugliness and value art, luxury and physical comforts. The native will possess strengths such as determination, persistence, modesty, tolerance and a balanced common sense. Such a native will avoid emotional hysteria or depression. The native is likely to possess all these qualities if he/she has a positive influence of Venus in his/her chart.

It is believed that the native's attitude and position relating to money and possessions are also connected to this planet. But how much of these characteristics the native can assimilate depends on the placement of Venus in the chart. We have already indicated in the previous pages that, irrespective of the placement of a planet in a horoscope, every planet rules certain signs. Coming back to our example of the person born on 3 March 1962, we would like to remind the reader once again how Saturn, sitting in the rising sign (ascendant), also governs the second house in the native's chart, as it is its ruler (Aquarius) too. Likewise, though it may be sitting in any house in a chart, Venus bestows benefits on a native according to the rising sign in a house and its ownership of the houses in a chart. For example, if it is rising in Virgo at the ascendant, it will rule the ninth as well as the second houses. Although its rising sign is weak, as Venus in Virgo is considered in its low ebbs, it is likely to bestow benefits from good luck and the native will earn good money from his profession. Venus is also associated with charm, aesthetic sense, pleasure, affection, partnership, harmony, money, possessions, sensuality and romantic love. Let us now identify the characteristics bestowed on the native on account of the rising and transiting of Venus in different Zodiac signs and in different houses respectively.

When Venus rises in Aries in a chart, it endows a person with passionate moods and makes him/her think mostly about love. The individual may fall in love quickly and like to demonstrate it as well. The native possesses great enthusiasm for sex and love and takes great delight in such matters. Such natives possess a strong force of passion to attain their goals, especially in love and romance, and make constant efforts in that direction. Although an element of selfishness may sometimes be visible in the native, he/she will be generous to loved ones. The native is quite enterprising and this element of risk-taking may cause financial problems. Although the native may have a second source of income, money usually slips through his/her hand easily.

When Venus transits the first house (ascendant), the individual may be easygoing in most respects. The individual will possess great charm to love and be loved by the partner. The native can move quite gracefully so he/she will be socially desirable, especially on account of his/her innate sympathy and kindness. But such a native is lazy at times and may like to converse in relaxed moods. The native may sometimes have weight problems, mainly because of not being active and mobile. The individual must take care of this inactivity, which occurs chiefly due to his/her being lazy. But when

Venus is in the first house, to a great extent it helps to boost the native's luck.

When Venus is in Taurus it tends to make a person truly loving and affectionate. The native will care a lot for loved ones. At the same time, he/she can also be a bit possessive at times. Although prone to jealousy at times, the native is also quite generous towards family and friends. Material possessions will be extremely important as they contribute to security and stability. Much hard work will be needed to achieve luxury and comfort. If it is possible to make money, the native will be keen to do so. The native will often possess a talent for music, general love for beauty, art and good living.

When Venus transits the second house its influence will be increased if placed in Taurus. The native would like to acquire that which brings material security and is aesthetically pleasing. The native will have great love of beauty and want to feel good so as to attract others. Such natives are possessive and consider loved ones their possessions. The native may be generous but he/she may also use it merely to show off. The native should guard against such tendencies to live in peace and harmony.

When Venus is in Gemini it makes an individual very lively and light-hearted. The native is also seen at times in a flirtatious mood. He/she largely enjoys the emotional way of life. The native loves to cultivate good friendships and keeps an intellectual rapport with the partner. It is also observed that an individual born in this sign may have more than one love relationship at a time. The native born with Venus in Gemini in the chart will feel a great need for both friendship and intellectual rapport within emotional relationships. Such a native will love making money and also possess great talent as a bargainer, usually for his/her own benefit.

When Venus transits in the third house of a native's chart, he/she will have an ability to communicate sympathetically and with mutual understanding to friends. The native will relish intellectual challenges in life and like to study areas considered difficult. The native will tend to socialise to a large extent and often love to entertain people. The individual will like to live a relaxed life although he/she will be quite alert mentally and love a stimulating environment. Such a native will be inclined towards literature and would like to travel a lot.

When Venus is in Cancer there is something intrinsically beautiful in the native. The person is often endowed with caring qualities of love and affection. It is also observed that the native often tends to worry about unnecessary things, especially in relation to the partner. Quite often the individual expresses a high level of emotions. For a happy life, the native needs to keep a check on this. Love and affection are greatly focused on the home by the native, who will love to spend a great deal of money to make the home comfortable.

When Venus transits the fourth house in a chart, the native loves the home and desires to make it look comfortable and beautiful. The native tends to spend significantly on children, which may spoil them at times. The native may have a great love for his/her mother and be under her influence for a large part of his/her life. A strong Venus in this house may bestow comforts in the form of servants, the luxury of personal vehicles and general happiness to the native.

When Venus is in Leo the native undertakes to fulfil his/her partner's desires. He/she may spend a great fortune for sheer enjoyment of their relationship. He/she will be quite generous in spending money as an expression of his/her emotions. Since Venus is in Leo, the sign ignites passions in the individual. It also makes the native express love very clearly but this expression will be genuine and positive. The planet will bestow the native great encouragement for developing his/her talents. At the same time, it may induce a tendency to be bossy. The placement of Venus in Leo can bestow large-heartedness and feelings of generosity, and can also provide him/her with the quality to enjoy all aspects of life.

When Venus transits the fifth house in a chart the native will possess great appreciation for the arts, music, fashion and painting. The native is likely to enjoy his/her romantic life. The individual will be fond of a luxurious and stylish life. If Venus is placed beneficially in the chart, the native may not indulge in financially risky activities. If it is not well placed, it may lead the native to indulge in gambling, causing him/her to overspend. The native must avoid financial games that carry risks, as it could be disastrous for him/her. If Venus is placed in the fifth house in an unfriendly sign, the native is likely to experience its bad effects in life.

When Venus is in Virgo it is in a debilitation state. It makes the individual low in emotions, and very critical of himself/herself. Such a person may possess inherent modesty and a shy demeanour. The native will communicate very well with the partner. He/she will be quite discriminating, rational and modest as well. It is necessary that the native should learn to relax. As it is not considered to be a very strong sign for Venus, the native may develop certain traits leading to stubbornness and lack of decision-making at the right opportunity. The native is advised to consider carefully before taking decisions.

When Venus transits the sixth house in a chart, the native will possess a deep desire to eat and drink lavishly. It may create a weight problem to a large extent. Most individuals born with Venus in the sixth house may love routine work over regular jobs. The native will largely dislike working in dirty conditions, except when such work is related to arts or aesthetic fields. Such a placement of Venus may mitigate its good effects if it controls good houses in a chart. For example, if Venus controls either the ascendant, or is the owner of the fourth house (by *ownership* we mean Taurus or Libra rising in those houses), it will affect the individual's productive abilities, work habits and reduce benefits from a good house and family.

When Venus is in Libra in a chart, it makes the individual extremely tender and romantic, kind and diplomatic. Such a native will like to have a permanent relationship quite early in life. This may lead to many problems, however, as the native may not be psychologically ready for a relationship at that early age. The individual will possess a great appreciation for beauty and arts. Venus is likely to endow the native with creative ability. The native possesses refinement and his/her creativity finds expression in music and fashion designing. Such expressions of creativity will greatly be rewarding to the person.

When Venus transits the seventh house the native has great desire to share his/her life with a partner. There is a possibility that the identity of the native may be submerged with that of the partner. This happens because the native loves his/her partner deeply and is ready to sacrifice everything to please him/her. For personal growth, the native must nurture his/her personality also.

When Venus is in Scorpio it is not supposed to be very well placed in this sign. Although the native may try hard, his/her relationship with his/her life partner may be adversely affected. The native can get possessive and jealous. For a happy and peaceful life, the native has to guard against such tendencies. Some of the ill effects of Venus may be lessened if the seventh house, which denotes good and bad relationship with the partner, has good aspects from beneficial planets like Jupiter or Mercury.

When Venus transits in the eighth house in a chart, very often, it increases the intensity of the native's passions and emotions. It may give rise to feelings of jealousy and lead to disruption of a relationship. The native's sex life is very good unless a weak Venus is placed in a malefic sign. The individual tends to indulge others' problems and thus brings disharmony to his/her own life. By tradition, it is considered one of the fortunate placements for inheritance. Such a native is quite shrewd, especially in matters relating to business and investment.

When Venus is in Sagittarius it tends to provide the native with energetic qualities in expressing love towards his or her partner. But the native is generally restless. In fact, it is not Venus' friendly sign and may cause the native to feel dissatisfied and unfulfilled. Thus, the individual experiences a lot of restlessness most of the time. Such an individual should not take his/her partner for granted. The native may have a good sense of fun and enjoyment.

When Venus transits in the ninth house the individual will possess a great need and love for travel. The native tends to travel abroad frequently. Romantic episodes may happen abroad. It is also quite likely that the native may marry someone from overseas and live abroad. The individual may also possess a wise attitude towards philosophical matters and like to live an idealistic and peaceful life. Sometimes a romantic relationship with a highly educated partner may also take place. Since it is the house of luck, and if its owner is well placed in the chart, the native will enjoy its fruits all the time, especially when grown up and living with the mate and family.

When Venus is in Capricorn it tends to make the individual express love in a very refined way. At times, however, the native may be cool in his/her expression of love. The native will be very caring and honest towards the partner and will like to do a lot for him/her. The native will do plenty of hard work to earn more money to spend and please the partner. The individual will gradually develop a terrific sense of pride and quite often show it off to his/her loved ones. The individual will also possess dynamic power in his/her personality to attract others.

When Venus transits the tenth house the native will have a good relationship with colleagues. The native will take great pride in his/her profession and be emotionally involved in it. It is quite likely that the partner may support the native's aspirations and devotion to work and help him/her grow in life. It is also possible that, at times, coping with great responsibilities may be hard for the native. Therefore, he/she must not take work casually or in a lazy manner, for it may lead to difficulties.

When Venus is in Aquarius it is considered a great placement for Venus. The native possesses a dynamic personality that attracts others. The native's tendency to remain distant from his/her partner will have a detrimental affect on the relationship. Such a native may also possess some intriguing qualities. But he/she will be very careful with friends and exhibit a lot of love and loyalty towards them. It will contribute to a deeper relationship with friends. Such a person will often look detached from emotions and stay cool, which may be good at times.

When Venus transits the eleventh house the native will enjoy a great social life, which will always be important for him/her. The native is likely to have many friends. The native will feel extremely happy to work for the community and will like to raise money to help the needy. If the owner of this house is placed in it or in the first, fifth or second house, the individual will be financially well off.

When Venus is in Pisces it is considered transiting in the exalted sign and bestows wealth, wisdom and a lot of happiness for the individual. The native will possess great affection and warmth for his/her partner. Such an individual will have occasional financial benefits from luck, will be able to take the initiative when required, may grab an opportunity at the right time and enjoy great success in life. The native's main areas of success are financial companies, accounts, business in goods related to fine arts, dramatics and areas of higher learning. He/she will possess great intuitive powers, which will help him/her find answers to most problems in life.

When Venus transits the twelfth house the native may prefer to keep his/her romantic life secret, more so as he/she is very shy. It may also lead the native to daydream, which can isolate him/her from others. Such a native may also turn to religion to escape sexual desires. Since it the house of waste, expenditure and losses, Venus's placement in this house cannot be considered good, especially if Venus is ruling (owns) any benefic house.

Transits of Mars

Mars is considered the lord of war in the astrological field and its signs represent the masculine element in both sexes. Both males and females who possess Mars' influence on them can be aggressive by nature and sustain heat and anger, which they sometimes exhibit in their conduct. People with strong Mars in their chart (*kundali*) have pioneering and leadership qualities. They also have a great urge to defend the weak. Such people sometimes make great leaders in the world if other beneficial planets also assist a strong Mars in the chart by their beneficial aspects on it, or on the ascendant at the time of birth. In general, Mars governs physical energy, assertiveness, action, sex drive, and impulsiveness. Mars is further connected with mechanical work, fire and the like. Additionally, Mars is associated with spontaneity and ambition. A beneficial Mars may always bestow great energy on the individual and inspire him or her to take the initiative in tasks the native desires to take up.

When Mars rises in Aries it is in its own sign. It is a fiery sign and denotes aggression and lack of patience. People who are governed by the influence of Mars possess a high level of physical energy. They don't often listen to other people's advice and are hardly influenced by others' opinions. Such persons often love to spend their energy in sports and other activities relating to physical exercises. The native with Aries in Mars will never lack enthusiasm. At the same time the native will hardly possess any patience and want to be on the move. The native is inventive, original and impulsive. Such a person is also accident-prone, may get hurt on the head and sustain minor cuts too. The native may also suffer from burns at times.

When Mars transits the first house it will bestow powerful energy on the native which, if used positively, will be very beneficial. It may cause the individual to be inclined towards sports or other physically demanding activities, helping him/her financially as well as socially. The native will possess a desire to win, and to be first is very important for the native. The native will have great will power but possess much less patience and more hastiness in actions and taking decisions. However, Mars placed in this house may bestow feelings of selfishness and self-centredness, which needs to be avoided to lead a peaceful life.

When Mars is in Taurus the native will possess a great desire for money, security, luxury and comfort. The native is down-to-earth but stubborn and determined. He/she can be picky and so needs to be forgiving. The individual born with Mars in this sign is often hardworking and likes to wait to see the fruits of his/her labour. The flow of energy is usually controlled and steady, but when the individual is roused in anger there will be a considerable show of wrath. The individual is persistent and advances towards his/her objectives carefully. He/she must exert proper control on physical activities.

When Mars transits the second house it will help the native acquire wealth and possessions. The native expresses emotions very passionately and will provide a great deal of sensual pleasure to his/her partner. Such natives will also be determined and backed by the physical energy provided by Mars. If Mars is sitting in Taurus, Cancer or Scorpio signs in the chart, the native is likely to have sudden bursts of temper.

When Mars is in Gemini the native starts many projects but is unable to finish them. Dealing with so many things at the same time leaves the native with little energy to complete them. It tends to make the individual lose interest, leaving tasks unfinished. The native is very interested in travelling and is often restless. The native is advised to try working hard to keep his/her interest alive and to keep busy. If this does not happen the native may feel restless and short-tempered.

When Mars transits the third house it creates an argumentative tendency in the native, who is frank in his/her opinions and does not mind airing strong feelings and views before others. The individual will possess a great sense of urgency and like to know the answers to questions immediately. He/she will highly be inquisitive and desire to know everything at once. Being the owner of the eleventh house, Mars rising in Gemini at the ascendant will be quite beneficial money-wise. However, being the owner of the sixth house, which is the house of sickness and disease, it may not be very helpful health-wise. In any case, it induces some kind of agility in the native, which keeps him/her moving towards his/her goals.

When Mars is in Cancer the native does not like to work, which appears difficult for him/her. Even a small task seems huge. The native is generally lethargic and likes to work at home, perhaps because he/she needs security around him/her. The native wants to be on his/her own but also needs family and friends close by.

In fact, Mars is in its debilitation sign in Cancer. So its impact on the individual can be of a different nature. The energy of Mars is expressed emotionally and passionately in this sign. There may be quite a lot of physical stress and tension for the native. The native's love and sex lives are powerfully influenced making him/her a very sensuous and caring partner. The native may possess a very short temper, and hurl some harsh and occasionally cruel remarks in moments of anger. The native must keep in mind that impulsiveness during bouts of anger should be bridled.

When Mars transits the fourth house the native may spend a great deal of energy on redecorating and improving the home. Some natives, with Mars in the fourth house, may like to move house a couple of times. The native may be highly influenced by the mother and not so much by the father, as the mother can be dominating. Mars can bring good results to the native in this house, provided its ownership is good.

When Mars is in Leo it makes the native outgoing, very attractive and dynamic. The native can easily influence people. The individual has a lot of creative energy, which makes the native choose careers like acting, drama or ones of a similar nature. But, at times, such a native is self-centred.

In fact, the fiery enthusiasm, energy and assertiveness of Mars are well represented in Leo. This placement of Mars in the chart gives the native great organisational abilities. If Mars is not influenced negatively by Saturn, it is quite likely that the native's sex life will be quite rewarding and colourful. The native will not like pettiness and small-mindedness. Though the native may possess a quick temper, he/she forgives and forgets just as quickly. The native needs to look after the heart and exercise regularly to keep fit.

When Mars transits the fifth house it may bestow an extremely rewarding romantic life. The native is likely to be an assertive lover. He/she will express passions positively. The native will take much pleasure in children. He may tend to take risks even in matters of life and have a tendency to gamble, which needs to be checked. He/she will have less patience in most matters relating to life. The individual will be generally enthusiastic about everything. This kind of placement of Mars may tend to make the native love sports and physical activities.

When Mars is in Virgo in a chart, it makes the native work very hard, without tiring for hours. At times, the native does not know when to stop working, such is the energy and impetus bestowed upon the native by Mars in Virgo. Rising in a sign governed by Mercury, besides energy, Mars may also bestow intellectual qualities. The native is, therefore, very smart and can plan things well. The individual likes order and good organisation at work. Since such natives feel they are very smart, they do not work well with others. But the native does not like to relax completely, which can lead to nervous stomach upsets and tensions.

When Mars transits the sixth house in a chart, it may provide some sort of nervous strength, more so if it is not conjoined with Saturn or seen by it. Such a native will be quite willing to work for others and be helpful. Although the native may not be quite satisfied with the daily routine, he/she would like to take up a job to help others and the self as well. If it is not the owner of the first, eleventh or fourth house, the placement of Mars in this house could be beneficial. If it owns the first house, it may bring disease or sickness, while ownership of the eleventh house may bring financial losses.

When Mars is in Libra it will not provide as much energy to the native as the other signs can provide. Such a native will want an easygoing and luxurious life with many possessions. The native would like others to wait on him and to be respected by all. He/she is a slow-moving but well-liked personality. The Libran tendency is to fall in love instantly and to want that state to last forever. This can cause problems for the native because things don't always happen as planned. When Mars is placed in Libra it may endow the native with excessive emotional temperament, which could be a problem for him/her, as emotions are not always reciprocated. The native must guard against such tendencies.

When Mars is placed in the seventh house it may not be good for the partner, from whom the native may have many expectations. Sometimes he/she will push the partner to such an extent that it may create problems for both. For a happy life, therefore, the native must not try too hard with his/her partner. Since Mars has a great bearing on the sex life of an individual, the native may give more importance and stress to it and consider sex vital. This could be detrimental to a happy married life. The native must keep an eye on that kind of tendency.

When Mars is in Scorpio it is its own sign. So Mars is in a strong position if its rising sign is within 8 to 16 degrees, and not in opposition to the ascendant. At times, the native makes a sudden and public show of emotions. The native works very hard and, when combined with qualities such as dedication and determination, he/she can reach the desired goals. Very often, such people reach the very top of the ladder. The native has the quality to influence others to a great extent. People always respect his/her determination and energy.

When Mars transits the eighth house in a chart, it bestows an extremely powerful sex drive. The native possesses a fascination for investigation and a great tendency to self-analyse. The native's choice of career can be influenced by the placement of Mars in the tenth, fourth or seventh house. The native may have great attraction towards surgery, psychiatry, police, or even detective work. The native may show great interest in finance and big business, with a keen and positive attitude towards investment. Before indulging in investments or such activities, the native must know whether Mars is sitting or transiting in a benefic sign in the chart.

When Mars is in Sagittarius the native tends to take up big and long projects, which he/she can hardly complete because they require a lot of time. The native loses interest in work after some time. The individual is very fond of sports and outdoor activities, which help to keep a check on his temper. The truth is that Mars provides the native great energy, due to which he/she moves very fast and at times even recklessly. It could be disastrous in many ways. Such natives always want to reach the top and can do so if they have patience and take on one project at a time.

When Mars transits the ninth house in a chart it may provide the individual with intellectual abilities and strength to accept intellectual challenges. The native will possess the power of concentration and tend to attain higher education. The native will be very fond of travelling and inclined towards jobs that involve travel. If Mars is placed in Pisces, the native will have sympathy and concern for others, and will be adventurous if it is in Capricorn and eccentric if it is in Aquarius.

When Mars is in Capricorn it is a great placement for it because it is in its exalted position in the sign. It will help the individual achieve great success in life, provided its placement is good in the chart. If it is placed in the ascendant, it will bestow colossal mental energy to the individual and make him/her construct big mansions and bungalows, provide great attachment towards mother and family, and bring great financial benefits from the age of 23. The native, though greatly influenced by Mars, will have the right amount of patience, which will be very beneficial at work. It makes the native highly responsible.

When Mars transits in the tenth house the individual will be considered a great force in his/her career and professional life. The native will possess a great ability to work hard and the potential to be a great success in life. The individual may be emotionally involved with his/her career, wanting to make quick progress. But hasty decisions and lack of tolerance of slower colleagues can cause problems, so the native needs to slow down to accommodate others. If Mars' placement is good in the chart, it may provide considerable enthusiasm for worldly progress, and ambition to achieve great positions.

When Mars is in Aquarius it makes the individual very cooperative, so he/she likes to work with others. The native often takes up jobs in big organisations. He/she has a very sensitive nervous system and possesses a great need for freedom. Often stubbornness is observed in the native, whose energy is mostly spent unevenly. Such natives may often be very polite and take care of others' feelings. But a tendency towards eccentricity in conduct may lead to tension and disruption in relationships. If Mars is well placed in the chart, the native may not like to hurt others and may possess a great desire to help most people. But being less practical, he/she may not be able to fulfil this.

When Mars transits the eleventh house it tends to make the native a great friend and his/her social life is highly rewarding. But the native will hardly like to be challenged in arguments, considers his/her opinions of great value, and doesn't accept any contradiction in that respect. It becomes a major reason for break in friendship, which the native values a lot. Still, a well-placed Mars in this position can benefit the native with money and fortune.

When Mars is in Pisces the native is endowed with quite low energy, which is frustrating to him/her at times. In fact, such a native is more a daydreamer rather than a practical person. It is difficult for him/her to make plans and if at all he/she makes one, it is not possible to carry this out. The best way for the native to progress is to be guided or pushed by others. Being very touchy, the native doesn't like to be pushed and has great self-esteem.

When Mars transits the twelfth house in a chart it can make the native very secretive, as he/she will keep information or problems to himself/herself. It may cause restlessness and confusion and consequently create problems for the native. The native may be involved in unfruitful travels and less beneficial activities, causing financial worries. But such a native will be a natural identifier of human ailments and suffering, for which he/she will devote much of his/her time, energy and money.

Transits of Jupiter

Jupiter is considered one of the most beneficial planets. It governs luck, happiness, progress and expansion. The largest planet in the solar system, it is related to physical and intellectual expansion of individuals. It is also associated with acquiring knowledge. It tends to develop one's philosophical outlook in life and encourages human understanding of other people and lands. When Jupiter is well placed in a chart, the native is mostly optimistic, broadminded and often directs mental energy very positively. The primary characteristics of Jupiter are expansiveness and good fortune. It adds to the native's fortune, which makes it a permanent benefic planet. It is also associated with religion, wealth and success. It is considered very positively placed when rising in a friendly or exalted sign in the ascendant. When it is negatively placed in a chart it can encourage blind optimism, extravagance and wastefulness, and can make the native showy.

When Jupiter is in Aries the native will have a strong and a positive view of life. But the native may be too optimistic at times and believe that all is going well, when it truly isn't. This may lead to disappointments. In order to avoid distress, he/she must weigh each situation carefully and be more practical. But the individual is certainly optimistic, besides being assertive, broadminded and enthusiastic on account of Jupiter's influence. The pioneering spirit of Jupiter may often surface in the individual's attitude and may be expressed through adventurous activities and a great desire for travel to faraway, unknown lands. It may also encourage sportsmanship and a competitive spirit, along with a philosophical outlook and an intellectual spirit. Such a native is largely an extrovert.

When Jupiter is transiting the first house and is closer to the ascendant, being 8 to 10 degrees nearer to the rising sign, its influence is very strong. It is an extremely powerful placement of Jupiter, which adds to a strong, positive outlook towards life. The native will be warm-hearted and optimistic. Such a placement of Jupiter brings every kind of affluence to the native. He is also often seen as a good-looking person outwardly and beautiful inwardly. He or she will have a breadth of vision and, if Virgo is rising at the ascendant, the native will also possess the ability to assess situations very wisely. The native is very open and honest and accepts others at face value. Such a native will usually have positive qualities, like encouragement of others. The native may also tend to possess a philosophical attitude towards life. There is a great ability in the native to develop intellectual ability. The individual should guard against obesity.

When Jupiter is in Taurus the native will often like to overdo things, especially in areas like eating, drinking or playing. The native accepts things as they are and does not like to see any change in them. That means the individual is an easygoing person and does not bother altering his/her ways. He/she just likes to take life as it comes. The native may be self-indulgent and tend to overeat. The placement of Jupiter in Taurus may motivate the native to make money. He or she will take great pleasure in entertaining others. If Jupiter is rising in Taurus, the native may lack warm-heartedness and a good outlook towards life.

When Jupiter is transiting the second house in a chart it may develop a great desire in the native to earn more money. He or she may like to invest a lot to earn as much as possible. Unless there is no aspect of Venus in it, the native can fulfil desires by hard work. The impact of Venus in any form, however, may turn the hopes into disaster as Jupiter and Venus are not natural friends. Such a native may not get as much in love as he or she desires. So he or she has to be very careful in this respect in life.

When Jupiter is in Gemini the native possesses a sense of humour. The native is naturally curious, which helps him/her grow and get good things in life. The individual is always desirous of adventures in life. He/she loves to travel and is eager to learn, although concentration is a problem at times. The native is desires to know too much too soon and so, he must learn to be patient. Jupiter is not so well placed in this sign, so it may cause intellectual restlessness, making the native fickle and, therefore, unable to make any progress. The individual may be broadminded but will lack in-depth knowledge. Still the placement of Jupiter in this sign may make one a good teacher, especially of young children.

When Jupiter transits the third house in a chart it will provide great enthusiasm in the native for intellectual development. The native may love to share his or her opinions and even impose them on others. The individual will be good at communicating with others. Jupiter may create a great desire to learn and to continue studies, even after schooling is over. The individual will have a great desire for physical and mental mobility. The native needs to be very careful when taking driving or riding lessons, and guard against an inherent wild streak.

When Jupiter is in Cancer it is considered one of the most important signs for the planet. The native is very optimistic and always likes to create more security for the family. Such a native is often very noble, proud, respected and loves justice. The individual will seldom feel dismayed and be ready to help the needy and the poor. He/she will like to share with others and is loved for this reason. As Jupiter is traditionally well placed in this sign, its positive influence is great on the individual. He or she will possess natural kindness, sympathy and understanding towards others. Such a native will be charitable, caring and protective, especially with the weak and the poor.

A humanitarian, the native will possess great creative ability. If it is placed in the 9th house of a native, it will bring tremendous good luck and he or she will certainly be a great literary person, as it will also be ruling the 5th house from that position. But if it is placed in the ascendant, it may bring more intellectual quality but less comfort from the partner, as its influence on the seventh house will be weak or not quite positive.

When Jupiter transits the fourth house a happy childhood is often predicted. Great benefits from mother and family life are expected, and the native may be in possession of a large mobile and fixed property. Such a native will tend to be generous towards the needy and will employ his/her energies towards fulfilling their requirements. Though the native may not be much inclined to earn money, his/her interests will continue in building property or extending such assets for the security of the family.

When Jupiter is in Leo the native possesses manly qualities, is brave, and ready to take the initiative in matters that need his/her attention. The individual is creative, dramatic and has a desire to be appreciated by people. Such individuals are mostly popular and like publicity. He/she always likes to give something to others and in this sort of disposition he/she is very sincere. Except when the native is in an unhappy mood, he/she never lets anyone down. When Jupiter is in Leo the native is full of optimistic zeal and enthusiasm, and possesses a great deal of generosity. He/she is intelligent and ambitious but at times showy in dress and behaviour, which may be the result of being an extrovert.

When Jupiter is transiting the fifth house, it will certainly bestow great enthusiasm and optimism. It may enhance certain talents in the native, especially painting and acting. Due to overenthusiasm, the native may sometimes be led into gambling. If this is true, he/she must try to divert attention to other fruitful activities. Such a placement of Jupiter can be a great source of encouragement to friends and family. Jupiter in this house may exert a powerful influence on the native's love life. He/she may have more than one partner in life, towards whom the native may show great generosity.

When Jupiter is in Virgo the native is good with details. The native will possess considerable literary skills and patience, as well as the dedication to be a good writer. This placement of Jupiter also contributes to technical and scientific ability and makes him act pragmatically. When the native takes any responsibility, he/she takes care of everything. The individual possesses good judgement and can foresee things. It is quite likely that the native may be prone to hasty decisions, which he must guard against. Being the owner of the fourth and seventh houses, if Saturn rises in Virgo at the ascendant, it will be very beneficial to the native in matters relating to family and the partner. The native will also have a lot of positive influence from the mother, if no malefic planet aspects the fourth or the seventh house.

When Jupiter transits the sixth house in a chart it tends to make the native sensitive to others' needs and feelings. As a result, he/she is quick to offer help. Too much work and too much food, or even too much inaction, can have a serious effect on the native. To lead a healthy and happy life, the native has to check some of these things.

When Jupiter is in Libra it is not quite a friendly sign for Jupiter. So the native must guard against being judgemental. Although such a native may be quite popular in public, there is something unique about his/her character, which doesn't make him/her act sincerely. It is still possible that such a native may do well in matters relating to marriage and other partnerships. The native may have problems from children and even friends as Jupiter, the owner of the third and fifth houses, occupies its enemy's (Venus) house in the ascendant. The native must guard against such matters to make life easier.

When Jupiter transits the seventh house in a chart it may transmit both good and bad influences on the native. From the Indian astrological point of view, Jupiter's sitting in the seventh house delays marriage and may create some problems for the native. The native tends to have relationships of that nature at an early age. However, there may be problems with the partner because the native's aspirations and generally high expectations aren't entirely met. As a result, perhaps the native gives up too soon. It is advisable, therefore, that the individual should give the matter serious thought before reaching any decision. What is more important is to act in accordance with the partner's needs.

When Jupiter is in Scorpio the native possesses deep faith in God and religion. The native loves secrets, of which he/she has many. The individual loves to take up challenges in life. Such an individual possesses deep interest in mysterious things, places and people. The native has a lot of pride and stands up boldly for what he/she believes in. In fact, Jupiter being in its friend's house and in a powerful sign, it will inject the native with its emotional energy and cultivate greater determination and will power in him/her. Jupiter will make the individual live life to its fullest. But the native must be careful against burning too much energy in the quest for pleasures only. The individual should try to avoid tendencies that develop suspicious feelings, as they often lead to jealousy and hatred. The native can be successful in writing detective fiction or develop such material if interested in writing. Research in criminal areas or a career as a lawyer could be rewarding.

When Jupiter transits the eighth house in a chart it may bestow financial gains through investments. The native should have a good business sense. The native also has a considerable sexual urge. The native will possess a freedom-loving element, which will be expressed very naturally and openly. Traditionally, Jupiter's placement in this house was considered to benefit the native with good inheritance but it may not be entirely true. For this, it is important to see which houses Jupiter controls in the chart and which planets influence it.

When Jupiter is in Sagittarius it makes the native very loving and understanding. Such a native is very wise and has natural luck on his/her side. The individual is greatly enthusiastic and loves travelling to foreign lands. But this desire can be fulfilled if there is someone to push him/her. Being a daydreamer, at times, the native leaves things half done. The mother or partner's role in this respect can be more beneficial to help the native realise his/ her dreams. But Jupiter being in its own sign provides the native with all those qualities that are bestowed on him by the Sun in this sign. The native may have some great intellectual potential, which may emerge in the later period of life. The individual may also possess a happy-go-lucky attitude. It may make him/her an adventurous, enthusiastic and risk-taking person.

When Jupiter transits the ninth house in a chart it tends to inject the native with considerable intellectual potential. His/her outlook in life is very positive and the vision very broad. The native's imagination will be backed by new ideas and love of travel. The native will always desire to acquire knowledge. The individual also possesses considerable versatility which, at times, causes him/ her to be restless. The native may also possess a flair for languages and like to live in foreign lands.

When Jupiter is in Capricorn it is a debilitation sign; therefore, it may not benefit the native much, except if it occupies a beneficial house and, at the same time, controls beneficial houses in a chart. Besides, the sign Capricorn, represented by the half goat, half fish, also has a great impact on the individual. Half of the native wants one thing, while the other half wants another. It results in doing nothing or doing very little. It is necessary that the native try and discover areas of interest and work accordingly. The planet may also provide the native with extrovert (Jupiter) and introvert (Capricorn) qualities. But the individual will be determined and not shirk responsibilities. The native will tend to work very hard and possess great powers of concentration. Such an individual will always be kind and thoughtful but sometimes he/she may start believing that he/she is always right.

When Jupiter transits the tenth house in a chart it provides the native with real strength to understand a situation very intelligently and vividly. He/she knows the long-term advantages of an event, situation and happening. The native is likely to acquire much worldly wisdom, which will help him/her reach his/her goals. The native will tend to seize opportunities to turn them in his/her favour.

This placement of Jupiter may make an individual showy and dramatic. Many actors and actresses often have this sign in their charts. There may be a talent for publishing or law in the native born with this sign.

When Jupiter is in Aquarius in the chart the native wants to be popular and, therefore, socialises a lot. For such a native, friends will be very important in life. The native cares about people, especially the downtrodden whom he/she will always be ready to help. Such a native wants a world without class, race or religion. But the native must not involve himself/herself in many matters that cannot be handled well. The native will have a splendid imagination and great originality when Jupiter rises in this sign in the chart. The native will also possess very powerful humanitarian qualities and express them in a very positive way. It is also observed that such a native is mostly impartial, tolerant, and sympathetic in an unsentimental way. He/she will possess great scientific or technological ability, which will be expressed through great imagination and originality.

When Jupiter transits the eleventh house in a chart it bestows great socialising ability. The native often gathers a large circle of friends and acquaintances, who contribute a lot to his/her circle. He/she may serve on various committees and hold important positions. The native possesses a natural inclination and ability to generate much energy and enthusiasm in others. The native in that respect will always be an excellent friend, encouraging others and helping them develop their potential. In matters of romance, however, the native needs to proceed with caution.

When Jupiter is in Pisces the native is very kind and considerate. He/she will care for others more than his/her own self. But the chances are that those whom he/she chooses to help may cheat the native. Such a native is happy in working with a group rather than on his/her own. But the native will be a private person, not willing to share his/her inner self with others to the extent that he/she may feel lonely in life many a times.

It has been observed that on account of the influence of the sign, Jupiter will bestow philosophical, spiritual and reflective elements in the native. That will develop a kind, sympathetic and caring attitude. The native will cultivate a compassionate spirit and a very

111

friendly attitude in life. It is observed that people who are working in the medical profession generally possess Jupiter in this sign in their charts. Such a native may also have abundant love for animals and will be prepared to help anyone who is in great need.

When Jupiter transits the twelfth house in a chart it may help cultivate a religious attitude in the individual. The native may possess a tendency to work in peace and alone. The native may have a philosophical attitude towards life. He/she may be a concrete worker, who devotes most time in some kind of creative work but all alone. In fact, much will depend on Jupiter's controlling particular houses in a chart. If it owns the fourth, ninth or any other benefic houses, the native will lose much of its beneficial effects as Jupiter has been placed in the twelfth house.

Transits of Saturn

It is a distant, slow-moving planet that attributes age and wisdom to humans. It takes 29.46 years to complete an orbit of the Sun. Traditionally, Saturn was said to rule both Aquarius and Capricorn but when Uranus was discovered, astrologers began to perceive a correlation between Uranus' influence in a chart and the traits of the sign Aquarius. Gradually rulership was assigned to Uranus.

Saturn is associated with time, age, and social order. It is considered an embodiment of stability, and the opposite of upheaval. Saturn is known as the taskmaster, on account of which it is taken to be the malefic planet in traditional astrology. It represents the conservative, self-controlled, security-seeking planet.

When Saturn rises in Aries it tends to make the native defensive, cautious and often afraid to take responsibility. The native goes on struggling inwardly, but when he/she decides to act, it may take time. The individual always tries to choose the best opportunity. It is absolutely important for the native to keep courage and be able to choose the right opportunities in life. Since it is the debilitation sign, in which Saturn is in its lowest ebb, the native has to be very cautious while moving forward.

When Saturn transits the first house in a chart, a great deal depends on how close to the ascendant it is placed, as far as its rising degrees are concerned. If it is within 10 degrees it is deemed to be in conjunction with the ascendant. It may cause shyness and lack of self-confidence in the individual. At the same time, it will bestow the qualities of caution and common sense. At other times, however, the individual may not be able to cope much with problems and responsibilities. It may be caused primarily due to lack of self-confidence. The native may be inhibited and possess a conservative outlook. This placement of Saturn may also cause a bad relationship with the father. Such a placement of Saturn predicts that, early in life, the native will not receive much help from the father.

When Saturn is in Taurus the native may take quite a long time in building the future, but he/she is patient, unlike someone born under the sign Saturn in Aries. Through hard work, the native saves money for the future. He/she may have some inclination towards the arts and may possess literary qualities, as Saturn is in Venus' sign, which is connected with arts and literature as well. Saturn also brings a tendency to be highly social. The native may be luxury-loving, but prudent in matters relating to life.

When Saturn transits the second house in a chart it may make the individual work very hard to earn money, and there isn't much hope for any sudden gains. So, whatever the individual gets as a result of hard work will be taken as a reward, bringing a lot of satisfaction. It will help boost the native's confidence and esteem. Placed in the second house in a chart, Saturn may infuse the native with emotions and is likely to create some sort of speech problems, especially if it is not in a friendly sign.

When Saturn is in Gemini the native tries to drive life with a quick pace but is not able to achieve expected results. The individual wants to possess much more than he/she has, which can lead to occasional frustration too. But the individual is quite smart and a good conversationalist. The native often tries to learn from his/her mistakes, but often has a hard time finishing what he/she has started. But the individual in whose chart Saturn is in Gemini will be highly intellectual and stable, and have a scientific temper. The native will speak less but wisely. It is therefore considered a positive sign for Saturn to be placed in Gemini.

When Saturn transits the third house it is considered a very powerful placement. This house is related to how much effort one will make in life, the positions and response from brothers, relationship with friends and social status. Besides, Saturn has aspects on the ninth house fully when it sits in the third house. Therefore, it may bestow so many qualities on the native, like making him/her dogged in nature, possessing a very friendly attitude, and being helpful to brothers and members of the family. But again such matters will depend on which houses Saturn rules in the chart. If it rules the first and second houses, or ninth and tenth or eleventh houses, its impact will surely be positive in the respects mentioned above.

When Saturn is in Cancer the native often tends to feel insecure. He/she tries hard to please others but, on account of his/her light tongue, may not be able to do so. Since Saturn is in the Moon sign, it makes the native suspicious of others. The tendency to worry is likely to increase and the outlook may be pessimistic if Saturn is in Cancer. The native is often critical in his/her approach and his/her way of thinking is mostly backed by irrational thoughts. The individual is often unable to take action due to lack of confidence. To be happy and successful in life, the native must try to see things from others' point of view.

When Saturn transits the fourth house in a chart it has been observed that the native has rarely received any help from his/her father in the early years. Perhaps the father was ineffective, or he was not there at all. As it is the Cancer-Moon house, it normally helps enhance the native's intuitional powers, which could be checked by Saturn's placement in this house. The native must understand that his/her intuitional power will be boosted with adequate use and proper effort.

When Saturn is in Leo it tends to make the native unsociable in his/her conduct. The individual also develops hostility against others, often without reason. It is rather an odd sign for the transit or rising of Saturn in an individual's chart. It is bound to provide some kind of weakness in one's conduct, leading the individual to practise untruth and disharmony against friends, and thereby make him unsociable. In general, unless other planets' aspects and placement have not been good in the chart, the native will hardly have others' trust if Saturn rises in Leo in a chart. The qualities of Leo will hardly emerge if Saturn governs this sign. The worst faults of the native could be autocracy and inability to accept limitations. Pride, rather than objective decisions, will precede. It may be a great cause for the native's downfall and lack of success.

When Saturn transits the fifth house it may have a bearing on the native's relationship with his/her father. As a parent, the native may push his/her children too much and may not give them much freedom on account of his/her dogmatic nature. It may lead to disharmony between him/her and the children. But the individual may possess some creative talent, which may be slow to develop. He must work hard to boost it for a better future.

When Saturn is in Virgo it tends to make the native very serious towards work and duty. It influences the native's determination positively, so that he/she gets what is desired. The native works very hard and is careful in doing everything. In fact, it is a very friendly sign for Saturn to transit, as in the next sign it gets exalted. Besides, it is Saturn's friend's sign. Therefore, it takes many qualities from Mercury and bestows them on the native, making him/her very agile, reflective and analytical. Adherence to routine and practical activity is always present with this kind of placement of Saturn. The native pays attention to detail and discharges his/her duty patiently and cautiously. It is certainly a very powerful placement of Saturn in this sign in a native's chart.

When Saturn transits the sixth house it may provide an ability to work very carefully and hard. But he/she may also be known to grumble about small matters, which will lead to dissatisfaction and restlessness in the native. He/she will not like much change, which may be due to lack of confidence. For a harmonious life, the native must try to transcend pettiness and an overcritical attitude.

When Saturn is in Libra it is traditionally a well-placed sign for it. The native will possess a natural sense of justice and will possess above-average sympathy and understanding towards other people. Very often, kindness and practical common sense are also present in the native, who also possesses tact and diplomacy. The individual is often impartial, flexible and fair in his/her outlook. If its placement in the chart controls good houses like the fourth and fifth, it is highly beneficial for the native. Saturn is supposed to be in exaltation in this sign, and thus, it bestows on the native financial and other material benefits. Its impact on the native makes him/her turn towards religion. Such a native likes orderly and well-organised things. The native has a deep desire that everyone should be treated fairly and justice should always triumph. The individual is very strong in his opinions and likes to get things done.

When Saturn transits the seventh house in a chart it may encourage a serious attitude towards a permanent relationship. The individual may not rush into marriage but, once committed in love, the native will be a constant and faithful partner. If Saturn is in opposition to the ascendant, commitment is often delayed. Many times, for deep-rooted, psychological reasons the right kind of relationship will not be formed at all. It may be caused on account of prestige or money and the native may take a purely calculating attitude towards marriage. Love and romance will be lacking in this kind of relationship. It may also cause poor communication between the partners. It may happen more when Saturn is in opposition to ascendant, Moon or Mars, or placed in the tenth or seventh house. If it is placed in the fourth house, it may develop a tendency to be discontented with the home.

When Saturn is in Scorpio it tends to make the native serious about his/her own self. He/she expects too much of himself/herself and others too. An individual born with this sign is secretive and too defensive at times. Quite often the native tends to act too soon, which lands him/her in trouble. Saturn also gives an element of dark and brooding intensity to the native. But if Saturn is in Scorpio, he/she turns out to be very shrewd. The individual may be fond of good food and wine, which may influence his/her future in the long run. The native is advised to think more before doing anything. It is also necessary for the native to be careful about his/her health. Certain bad habits, especially overeating and drinking, may have an adverse effect on it.

If Saturn transits the eighth house in a chart, determination and good power of concentration are likely to be the best qualities that a native may possess. The native's outlook is often serious, and may have a tendency towards depression. This placement of Saturn may be good for those who carry financial responsibilities for others. But when Saturn transits in Scorpio, a rewarding and fulfilling sex life is not predicted. The native may possess fascination for the dark sides of life. He/she may also be suspicious and untrusting of others – too often towards the partner. He/she must employ caution in this respect.

When Saturn is in Sagittarius it tends to make the individual ambitious. The native might get involved in foreign matters. He/she is also very liberal in religious matters and interested in different religions. Sometimes the native does not get along with his/her kith and kin. The native also tends to care about others but does not like to interfere with their lives. Such individuals are proud of their own selves and have self-respect. But Jupiter and Saturn are essentially polar planets, for Jupiter represents expansion and Saturn indicates restriction. Thus, Saturn's placement in Sagittarius is not very fruitful. But Saturn accelerates concentration, and encourages the desire to study. It helps to develop the native's intellectual potential. In fact, Saturn in this sign may bestow on the native an insight with which he/she can see deep-rooted things clearly. It can also cultivate honesty and straightforwardness in speech and the native may air his/her opinions quite fearlessly. But this needs to be restricted to avoid ill feelings and misunderstandings.

When Saturn transits in the ninth house in a chart it may bestow the ability to think deeply and seriously about important issues of life. The individual may take up challenges with great caution. In case Saturn has negative aspects from other planets, it may produce shyness and lack of confidence in the native. This may result in an inferiority complex, especially when the native gets the opportunity to mix with people who are intellectually and academically superior to him/her. The native needs to make conscious efforts to lessen this inability to push him/her forward.

When Saturn is in Capricorn the native has a strong desire for power. It can make him/her quite rough and tough, as well as selfish. Consequently, the native ends up being unhappy. But such a native has the ability to plan. The individual wants to be successful and desires recognition. As it is Saturn's own sign, it does provide the native some kind of confidence with which he/she can reach desired goals. Saturn in Capricorn also provides caution, determination, ambition and practical ability. Sometimes the individual will make too many personal sacrifices to achieve objectives. The hardworking parent will do everything to give a better education and life to his/her children. But the native may be strict towards children. This needs to be curtailed and more freedom provided to them. The native is advised to keep moving to avoid stiffness in his/her joints.

When Saturn transits in the tenth house in a chart it is in its own house so its strength and influence is great. The native will be able to shoulder the many responsibilities he/she has. Sometimes the native may remain too busy with his/her work and be distant from his/her loved ones. It may result in loss of family love and disappointments. If Saturn is in its own sign it will certainly provide the native quite a good opportunity for jobs and position. Many times this leads the native to become a lawyer and helps him/her rise in it. The native must avoid getting too involved in his/her work, as it may lead to problems in his/her relationship with a partner or loved ones. Saturn in Capricorn or Aquarius signs in this house is highly favourable to the native.

When Saturn is in Aquarius it tends to make the native more social. The native likes to help people and serve them as much as he/she can. The individual considers friends very important, even more than his/her own self. This helps the native make a lot of friends. However, the native must refrain from doing things just to please friends. In any case, it is an interesting and positive sign for Saturn. It bestows on the native considerable determination, which is shown by the achievement of objectives. The native's mind possesses a strong element of originality, which at times may lead to rigidity. Saturn in this sign may also provide humanitarian qualities and a scientific temper, which may be increased if Saturn is in the ascendant or the ninth house.

When Saturn transits the eleventh house its influence on the native is quite positive as it helps him/her to improve finances and boost social prestige. The native may have a few close friends, who may be quite distinguished intellectually and be more worldly wise. A powerful humanitarian feeling will impel the native to work for people, especially those who are troubled and have met with injustice. But if Saturn is in Aquarius, it may have a bad aspect on the native's ascendant, making him cunning and quarrelsome, besides giving rise to frequent negative thoughts. It may cause the native to be dishonest, which may bring him/her a bad name.

When Saturn is in Pisces the native tends to choose more than one career. Such a native tends to be scared of others' opinions and likes to withdraw on account of people's criticism. But the native is often desirous of serving people. Such a native may be involved in charity work. As Saturn is in Pisces, which has dual characteristics, it is quite likely that the individual may also be involved in two kinds of activities. This may involve serving people in one case and staying away from them on account of their criticism in another. The native is humble and sympathises with the needy. The individual may lack self-confidence and will be inclined to hold himself/herself back. Sometimes Saturn in this sign may induce feelings of depression, which must be kept in check.

When Saturn transits the twelfth house in a chart it may make the individual retreat from worldly matters and stay locked in his/her own world. It may also make him/her an introvert, which is harmful for personal growth. If Saturn conjuncts the ascendant in this house it may induce feelings of inferiority and may influence him/her to take part in some kind of undesirable, anti-social activities, which could be criminal at times. The native is advised to employ caution when taking decisions to act in the fields that don't interest him/her much. Impulsive behaviour must be kept in check. In this house Saturn may help the native check his/her extravagance as the twelfth house is related to expenses. Yet, the native may involve himself/herself with unnecessary expenses. Keeping this in view, the native must exert efforts to check such tendencies.

Transits of Uranus, Neptune & Pluto

Uranus governs friends, changes, original thoughts and humanitarianism, Neptune governs intuition, inspiration, dreams and fear, while Pluto controls the subconscious mind, and the ability to overcome difficulties. Both Neptune and Pluto move extremely slowly and take more than a hundred years to go through the Zodiac once. Millions of people are born when Neptune and Pluto are in the same sign. Astrologers, however, have not made any conclusive discovery about their effects on human beings. Some conjectures have been drawn but they are not very helpful. Of course, there is some information on Uranus' effect on humans but that too is not conclusive.

In fact, astrology is based on scientific procedures. It can be understood and known more by constant pursuit, deep desire to know more as well as by one's not becoming prejudiced on account of some kind of fragment of knowledge or information that he/she has already gained from a particular source in the past. What we mean is that, to get anywhere close to the truth, one has to keep learning. One way to do this is to examine as many charts (*kundalis*) as one can find. **We have, therefore, provided a number of charts (case histories) and analysed them for the readers' reference in the next chapter. In view of the importance of the planets' placements in various houses, their rulership of the houses, aspects on the planets and the houses, importance of the ascendant, ninth and tenth houses, the charts are analysed thoroughly.** Kindly read each chart very carefully and try to understand how we have analysed it, especially in view of the above factors.

Astrologers may differ in their approach in analysing a chart and may quote ancient texts justifying their predictions. They may be right to a large extent. In our opinion, however, the best way is to use all the experience and information one has gathered over years of personal observation, analysis and reflection. The ancient sages also applied the same methods, collecting information and writing it for us. Let the knowledge of those revered holy men be our guide. At the same time, our personal discoveries on the way must also form an important source of knowledge towards learning more in that direction.

In the next chapter, we have tried to provide something of that nature for the reader. Should you find that we have erred somewhere, and that your own conclusions are contrary to ours, kindly let us know so that we may correct ourselves.

Chapter Four

Aspects & Interpretations

Points to Ponder

If you want to be a good astrologer and analyse a chart correctly, you need to take special care and thought. To be on the right track, before one analyses a chart, it is important to keep certain principles in mind. There will always be exceptions and predictions will not be absolutely accurate all the time. If you proceed with care, however, you may not have to face disappointment and failure. Therefore, you must consider a few things before you make any predictions about anyone's chart. Keep in mind the placements and transits of the planets in different houses and signs. The third chapter of this book is mainly devoted to this. Besides, the characteristics relating to the ascendant, fourth, fifth, seventh, ninth, tenth and eleventh houses should also be kept in mind before reaching a definite conclusion.

You should also be mindful of the *Vimshottari dasha* that is operating at the time the chart is being analysed. *Vimshottari* is determined from the sign of the Moon being in a particular *nakshatra* at the time of one's birth. The Moon stays in one sign for two and a half days. So whatever degrees the Moon has transited in a sign when one is born, the *Vimshottari dasha* starts from that point. The Moon's degrees that have passed are considered *bhukta* years (years that have gone), and the remaining degrees form the *bhogya* years (the years not yet gone) in a particular *dasha.* Please see Table 4:3 to determine which planet's *dasha* would operate at one's birth in view of the *nakshatra.* To ascertain the correct *Vimshottari dasha*, you need to thoroughly study and understand the standard Indian calendar (*Panchang*). This calendar will assist you in calculating the appropriate period of *Vimshottari* operating at the time of the birth of a child. Some of these considerations, including the following important tips, must be kept in mind while making predictions. It is imperative for a

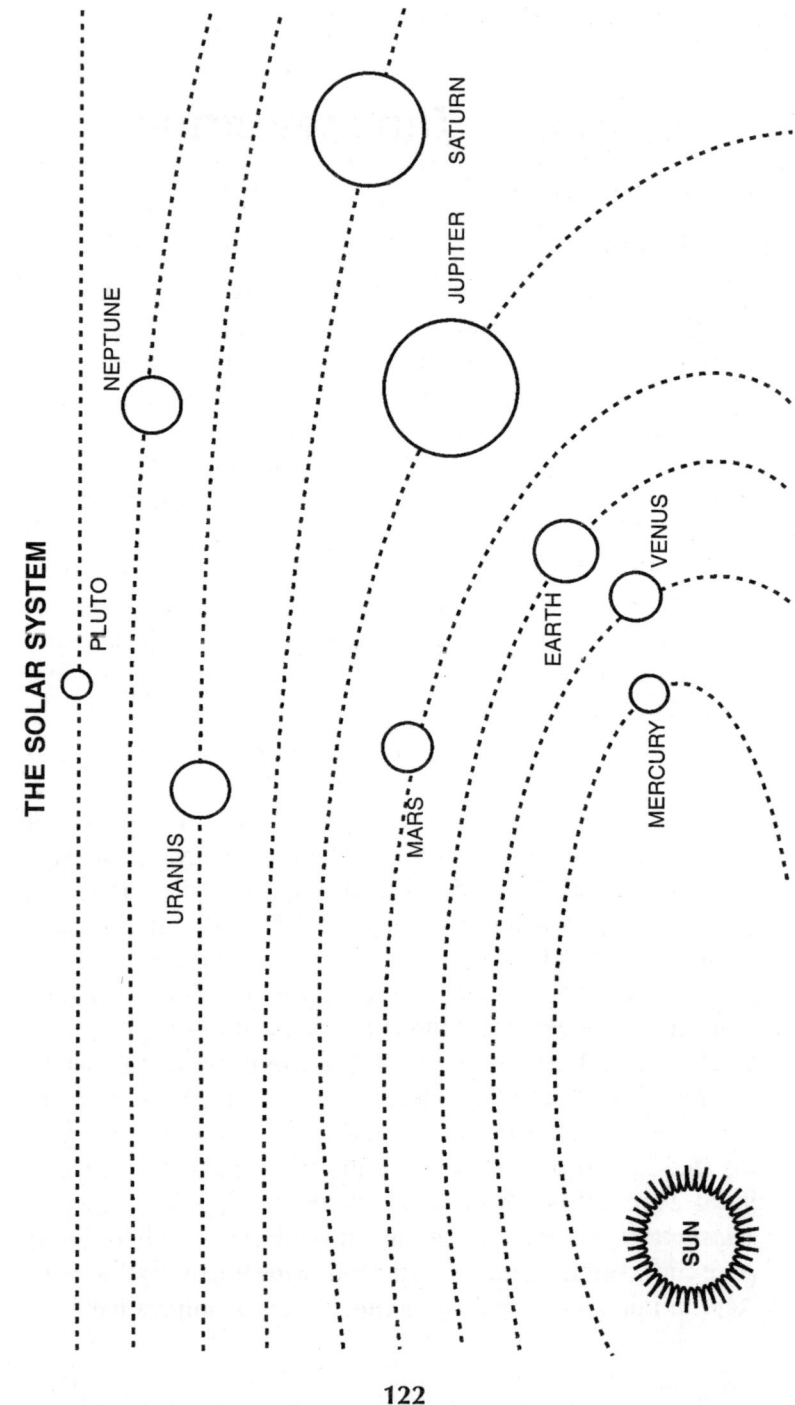

THE SOLAR SYSTEM

PLUTO

NEPTUNE

URANUS

SATURN

JUPITER

MARS

EARTH

VENUS

MERCURY

SUN

122

practising astrologer to remember what each house is meant for, and what will be the impact of a conjunct, aspect and placement of a planet in a particular house. Therefore, it is important to remember the following:

1. **The ascendant:** A comprehensive study of the rising sign in the ascendant will help you to reckon the native's characteristics, motivation, enthusiasm, assertiveness and other areas of personality.

2. **The Sun signs:** These will provide clues about how the native will express himself/herself at work and in terms of his/her career.

3. **The Moon sign:** It enlightens one about how the native will react in certain situations and what will be her/his emotional reactions when faced with difficult situations.

4. **The aspects:** It will help in understanding the strength of the houses and enable you to know how powerful the planet occupying a house is.

5. **Fourth house:** Its study will help you to learn about the position of the native's property, mother, servants, possession of vehicles and transport facilities, as well as the direction he/she may follow for settlement.

6. **Fifth house:** Its study will help you find out about the native's education, love affairs, number of children, productivity and similar issues.

7. **Seventh house:** Its study will help you know how efficiently the native copes with his/her boss, whether he/she will sail smoothly with the partner and what sort of partner will bring happiness to the native.

8. **Eighth house:** It will enable you to find out about the native's health. It may also give clues about longevity and span of his/her life. At times this house is also considered meaningful for acquiring hidden wealth and physical strength.

9. **Ninth house:** Study of this house will enlighten you about the native's social status, luck, travels and foreign tours.

10. **Tenth and eleventh houses:** These will enlighten you about the native's profession and sudden gains.

11. **Twelfth house:** This is mainly related to expenses, waste, travels as well as *moksha*.

12. **Transits of planets:** It will reflect on the native's creative abilities. For example, when Capricorn is rising, or if the Sun is in Leo, it may provide such qualities. A powerful Venus may suggest talent in music.

13. **Practical ability:** When certain signs like Capricorn, Virgo and Leo rise at the ascendant, they suggest practical ability in the native.

14. **Profession:** Planets such as Mars, Saturn, Jupiter, Mercury and Venus indicate a particular bent of the native's mind and help him/her choose a vocation these planets rule. For example, Mars rules sports, medicine, police and military; Saturn rules justice and law; Jupiter rules education and acting; Mercury indicates education and vocations related to public speaking and business; Venus rules arts, music and art-related vocations; and a combination of Mars with Saturn indicate engineering and architecture, etc.

Ownership of Planets

Besides the important points referred to above, there are other important aspects of astrology – the influence (aspect) of transiting planets on a native's life from their positions and placements in the chart, as well as their ownership of the houses. A planet is the owner of certain houses, which it controls totally, irrespective of its placement in a chart. For example, traditionally Saturn being the owner of Capricorn and Aquarius, it will control these two signs and the houses in which those signs rise in a chart, even if Saturn is transiting or sitting in the sixth, seventh, ninth or any other house.

What is crucial for the reader to know is how powerful and weak the particular houses are in a chart. Here, 'powerful' and 'weak' refer to how beneficial or malignant the houses are in terms of bestowing benefits and losses respectively. The extent of strength of a house is known from the aspects (look) of the planets on a particular house and from the degrees (out of 30 degrees) with which a rising sign is rising in a particular house. By degrees we mean how much time was left, out of two hours, for the rising sign when the native was born.

In fact, each planet has some kind of aspect on certain houses in a chart. What is that aspect and what is the effect of the planets' aspects on a house/planet or a native? This kind of knowledge is absolutely imperative for the reader, and he/she needs to comprehend it very carefully before trying to analyse any horoscope.

The Aspects

The term *aspects* refers to the angles between the Sun, Moon or planets and the earth, as they occur in the Zodiac at a particular time. In the second chapter, we have already considered how many angles can be formed within the circle or a rectangle that is drawn to make a chart of a native at the time of birth. However, we will discuss it again from some Western astrologers' point of view. They reckon that there are six important angles, out of which four are usually considered favourable, and two are unfavourable. These are:

(i) **Conjunction:** It takes place when two planets on the same side of the earth are nearly aligned with it, forming no angle with the earth, and sit in conjunction. On the native's chart (*kundali*) the planets are in the same sign and are also in conjunction. This position is generally considered a favourable influence, depending on the planets involved. Let us take in view the chart of the native born on the 3 March 1962 for this example, discussed in the second chapter. Both Saturn and Mars, though opposite in qualities and nature, are sitting in the ascendant in the chart (besides other planets), forming a great benefic (*yogkarak*) combination.

(ii) **Trine:** When planets form an angle of 120 degrees with the earth, establishing two points of a perfect triangle on the chart, it is considered highly favourable in all aspects. Signs that are four signs, or 120 degrees, apart from each other on the chart have the trine relationship. Different charts (*kundalis*) containing such combinations are analysed in this chapter for the reader's reference.

(iii) **Sextile:** When planets form an angle of 60 degrees from each other on the chart, they are said to be in a sextile position. This angle is a subdivision of the trine and also considered very favourable.

(iv) **Semi-sextile:** Planets forming an angle of 30 degrees on the chart are semi-sextile. This angle is considered quite favourable.

(v) **Opposition:** When planets are nearly on opposite sides from each other, and sit in 180-degree angles with the earth, they are said to be in opposition. This kind of aspect may not always be very favourable.

(vi) **Square:** Planets forming an angle of 90 degrees with the earth, and the signs that are 90 degrees apart on the chart, are said to be in square position. This angle is mostly considered unfavourable.

Many astrologers differ in their opinion about interpreting angles that are close but not quite exact. Some hold that a conjunction or opposition should be within one or two degrees to be considered, permitting about five degrees for other aspects. While there are others who reckon that when planets are within approximately 8 to 10 degrees from each other, they can be considered good for such aspects.

The above description of the planets' aspects is good from the Western astrological point of view but Indian astrologers have their own views on this. The big point of difference from the Indian astrological point of view is that most aspects can provide good effects, provided they are friendly and caused by beneficial planets only. But if a malefic planet makes an aspect on a good house or a benefic planet, it may have a bad impact on the native as far as a particular house is concerned. Through the following table, we are submitting the planets' aspects on different houses from the Hindu or Indian astrological point of view.

Table 4:1

Planets' Aspects on the Houses

Planets	Aspects on the houses
Jupiter	fifth, seventh & ninth
Mars	fourth, seventh & eighth
Mercury	seventh
Sun	seventh
Moon	seventh
Venus	seventh
Saturn	third, seventh & tenth

Since Neptune, Pluto, and Uranus are quite recent discoveries, the effect of their aspects has not been analysed much by most astrologers. However, it is broadly considered that these newly discovered planets have just one aspect, if any. They aspect only the seventh house from their positions in the chart.

We have already discussed some *important basics* relating to understanding astrological knowledge in the second chapter of this book. The basics that we have considered important so far are: What is a rising sign? How do you ascertain the rising sign in a chart? What are the qualities that an ascendant can bestow on a native? And, what qualities or characteristics a house bestows on an individual, including the meaning that can be drawn from the planetary positions placed in different signs and transiting in different houses of a chart? If that much has been understood well, it will benefit you in understanding a chart as well as conceiving how planets' aspects, conjuncts and placements influence an individual.

Some additional information will be given to the reader in this chapter, about how to read a chart. In view of that, a **number of case studies have been presented in testimony for your reference and information**. It will help to add new dimensions relating to astrological knowledge, which may benefit you in comprehending some very important characteristics of the planets, the effects created by their placement in a particular house, and various *yogas* (conjunctions) that may have occurred due to the planets' positions in a chart. If you can view all this very objectively and really desire to learn astrology without keeping any financial benefits in mind, you will surely be able to comprehend much about it.

Please keep in mind that the field of astrology is so wide and deep that one lifespan may not be enough to learn everything. Still, if you try hard, you may know enough to help a native when he/she needs your help at a difficult time. We don't claim to know everything about astrology but our humble efforts in explaining certain *yogas* (combinations), aspects and conjuncts created by the planets in a chart will be quite unusual and will, hopefully, enlighten the person desirous of learning astrology. Before presenting a chart for analysis, we would like to remind you once again about the planets' exalted and debilitated positions. Much depends on it when you try to analyse a chart and want to measure the strength of the houses in it. It is also necessary to understand the aspects of the planets on the houses and planets.

The table, relating exalted and debilitated positions of the planets presented in the second chapter, is being presented once again for your ready reference. Western astrologers also confirm the information referred to above, which is contained in **Appendix 2**.

Table 4:2

Planets' Ownership, Exalted and Debilitated Positions

Planets	Ownership (Symbols)	Exalted Position	Debilitated Position
Sun	Leo	Aries	Libra
Moon	Cancer	Taurus	Scorpio
Mars	Aries, Scorpio	Capricorn	Cancer
Jupiter	Sagittarius, Pisces	Cancer	Capricorn
Venus	Taurus, Libra	Pisces	Virgo
Mercury	Gemini, Virgo	Virgo	Pisces
Saturn	Capricorn, Aquarius	Libra	Aries

In fact, it would not be enough to know the planets' exalted positions given in the above table. It is also necessary to know that each planet is exalted in a *rashi* only when it is transiting through a particular degree. The following chart will clarify it absolutely.

Table 4:3

Degrees in which Planets are in their Exalted or Debilitated Positions

Planets	Sun	Moon	Mars	Mercury	Jupiter	Venus	Saturn
Exalted Degree	0 10	1 3	9 28	5 15	3 5	11 27	6 20
Debilitated Degree	6 10	7 3	3 28	11 15	9 5	5 27	0 20

The above chart indicates that even if a planet is transiting in its exalted sign, it may not be considered exalted (but would be taken to be in its own *rashi* only) if it is not transiting in the right degrees. For example, the Sun in Aries will be considered exalted only when it is transiting in 0:10 degrees. So is the case with the other planets and their debilitated positions as well. The above information is absolutely imperative for the reader if he/she wants to predict correctly.

Vimshottari Mahadasha

Our knowledge about predictive astrology will remain inadequate if we don't discuss the importance of Mahadasha, such as Asttotari, Yogni and Vimshottari, etc. There are 52 dashas of this kind. *Vimshottari dasha* is more popular among all and is widely considered for calculating various incidences in one's life. These include education, marriage, time for job opportunities, possibility of death, birth of a child, benefits and losses during the lifetime of a native, etc. The following chart will enable you to understand how *Vimshottari dasha* (periods) operates in one's lifetime.

Vimshottari Dasha (years) controlled by each Planet

Nakshatra	Kritika Uttra Falguni Uttra Sha.	Rohini Hasta Shravan	Mirgshira Chitra Ghnishtha	Punarvasu Vishaka Purva- bhadra	Ardra Swati Shatb- hisha
Years owned by the Planet	Sun 6 years	Moon 10 years	Mars 7 years	Jupiter 16 years	Rahu 18 years

Nakshatra	Pushya Anuradha Uttra Bhadra	Ashlesha Jeshtha Revati	Magha Mula Ashwani	Purvafalguni Purvaashada Bharni
Years owned by the Planet	Saturn 19 years	Mercury 17 years	Ketu 7 years	Venus 20 years

The total span of the nine planets comes to 120 years. To learn more about the *Vimshottari dasha* system, you need to study more from other sources and keep your mind open when analysing a chart. In fact, making predictions involves many other things. We have already drawn your attention to some of these very important aspects of astrology under the subheading **Points to Ponder**. It will be rather impossible to make a final and correct prediction without remembering all these points listed above. If you wish to make correct predictions on the basis of *Vimshottari dasha*, you should remember that the placement of a planet whose *dasha* is operating in the chart is highly important. For example, if the *dasha* belongs to the owner of the ascendant, which is sitting in the first, fourth, fifth, ninth, tenth or eleventh houses, the results will always be related to those houses.

A concrete example will highlight this issue properly. Say for example, in a native's chart the Mercury *dasha* (17 years) is operating at the time you have examined the chart. If Mercury is the owner of the ascendant and is sitting in the first house, it will enhance the prestige of the native and give him/her financial and status-specific benefits. The native will enjoy great reputation and get support in his/her working place. If Mercury is sitting in the fourth house, it will give him/her benefits relating to property, motor

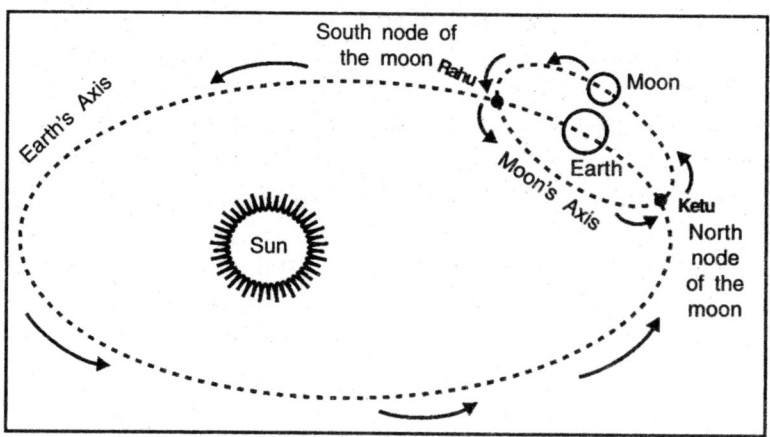

vehicle, love and support from the mother. He/she will also acquire a great residence. The native may be involved in buying land and property as well. If Mercury is sitting in the ninth house, it will enhance his/her luck, providing great opportunities for new jobs and travelling to foreign lands. It may give him/her financial benefits and recognition in the country and overseas as well.

Thus, during the Mercury *dasha* (period) the native will get great benefits provided its placement is in a beneficial house and/ or it is in conjunct with the owner of the ninth, fifth or eleventh. The native will enjoy all such benefits gradually, throughout the *dasha* and *anthra dashas*. But if the owner of the ascendant is sitting in the twelfth, eight or sixth house (at birth, we also call it nativity), the results will not be favourable. The more charts you examine carefully, you will feel more equipped with respect to the effects of a particular *dasha* operating in a chart. Please see **Appendix 3** for duration of various *dasha*, *bhukti* and *anthra* in *Vimshottari dasha*,as well as the cumulative periods in it.

In relation to the *Vimshottari dasha* you should remember that except the Sun and the Moon, which own only one *rashi* or sign (Leo and Cancer respectively), the other planets controls two signs. This is already stated in this chapter in Table 4:2, where we have also mentioned the planets' exalted and debilitated positions. Thus, while predicting, you should remember this fact and also keep in view that Neptune, Uranus, and Pluto are not included in *Vimshottari dasha* calculations, as not much is known about these planets so far. Therefore, only nine planets (including Rahu and Ketu) are considered to calculate *Vimshottari dasha*.

There's one more point that readers should keep in mind while making predictions. The transits of the major planets, such as Jupiter and Saturn, must be considered before predictions are made. Such transits and the aspects of the planets are highly important in making predictions. Rahu and Ketu are not the owners of any signs. They provide beneficial or unfavourable results on the basis of the signs they occupy in a chart. But these two nodes are highly favourable when they sit in the sixth, eighth, twelfth or even third house, especially in the signs governed by Saturn, Mercury or Venus.

Let us now discuss another very important aspect of astrology, which should always be kept in view when predictions are made – the conjunction of various planets in different houses, forming *Rajyogas*.

Rajyoga

There are several combinations that form Rajyoga in a *kundali* or chart. Some of them are quoted here from Laghu Parashari as well as deduced by the authors from their long experience in the field. You may verify the effects of some of the following combinations that make Rajyoga in the charts (*kundalis*) discussed here. For that purpose, everything depends on how much you remember the following conjunctions that form Rajyoga and benefit the native by its presence in the chart. Rajyoga simply means to enjoy benefits, facilities, riches and positions like that of a Raja or King. An IAS officer, a great businessman, a doctor, an engineer, a notable sportsman of international repute, a notable cinema star, or a highly devoted person known for his/her religiosity throughout the world, must possess certain conjunction of planets in the chart to make him/her reach that position.

Let us discuss some of those yogas known as Rajyogas to learn more about astrology.

1. The owners of the 9th and 5th houses (known as *mooltrikona*) and the owners of the 1st, 4th, 7th or 10th houses (known as *kendras*), when they own houses among these ones, become beneficial (*yogakarak*). For example,

132

if Aries is rising in the chart, the Sun and the Moon own the 4th and 5th houses. If both are sitting in the 1st, 4th, 5th, 9th or 10th houses, Rajyoga is formed. That means the *jatak* or native will enjoy all the benefits of a king.

2. If Taurus is rising in a chart and the owner of the 9th and 10th houses (Saturn) is conjunct with the owner of the 5th house (Mercury) in any of the *kendras* or *trikonas*, Rajyoga is formed.

3. When Gemini is rising in a chart, and the owner of the 1st and 4th (Mercury) is conjunct with the owner of the 10th (Jupiter), or conjunct with the owner of the 5th (Venus), it forms Rajyoga.

4. When Cancer is rising in a chart and the owner of the 1st house (Moon), and owner of the 5th and 10th (Mars) is conjunct in a *kendra* or *trikona*, they form Rajyoga.

5. When Leo is rising in a chart and the owner of the 5th (Sun), and the 4th, and 9th (Mars) are conjunct in a *trikona* or *kendra*, Rajyoga is formed.

6. When Virgo is rising in a chart and the owner of the 1st and 10th (Mercury) is conjunct with the owner of the 4th and 7th (Jupiter), or conjunct with the owner of the 2nd and 9th (Venus) in any *kendra* or *trikona*, Rajyoga is formed. If Mercury and Venus are conjunct in the 3rd house in this *lagna* (ascendant) and looks at the 9th house, it also forms Rajyoga. The native born on 1 January 1933, whose reference has been given under Vipreet Rajyoga at a later stage, has Virgo rising in his chart. Both Mercury and Venus are conjunct in his chart in the 3rd house. Consequently, he has never (until the age of 70 years in 2003) been out of job/work even after his retirement 12 years ago in 1991. There is also Vipreet Rajyoga in the chart as Mars, the owner of the 8th, is sitting in the 12th house.

7. When Libra is rising in a chart and owner of 4th and 5th (Saturn) is conjunct with the owner of the 5th (Mars), or with the owner of the 9th (Mercury), or with the owner of the 10th (Moon) in a *kendra* or *trikona*, Rajyoga is formed.

8. When Scorpio is rising in a chart and the owner of the 5th (Jupiter) is conjunct with the owner of the 9th (Moon), or with the owner of the 10th (Sun) in a *kendra*, Rajyoga is formed.

9. When Sagittarius is rising in a chart and the owner of the 1st and 4th (Jupiter) is conjunct with the owner of the 5th (Mars), or with the owner of the 10th (Mercury), or with the owner of the 9th (Sun) in a *kendra* or *trikona*, Rajyoga is formed.

10. When Capricorn is rising in a chart and the owner of the 1st (Saturn) is conjunct with the owner of the 5th and 10th (Venus), or is conjunct with the owner of the 7th (Moon), Rajyoga is formed. A clear example of this kind can be observed in the chart under **Case Study Two**, later in the chapter.

11. When Kumbha is rising in the chart and the owner of the 1st house (Saturn) is conjunct with the owner of the 4th and 9th (Venus) in a beneficial house, such as *trikona* or *kendra*, Rajyoga is formed.

12. When Pisces is rising in a chart and the owner of the 10th (Jupiter) is conjunct with the owner of the 4th and 7th (Mercury), or the owner of the 9th (Mars) is in a beneficial house, Rajyoga is formed.

In his *Jotishtatwa Viveka*, Ramesh Upaddhya indicates four more kinds of yogas that are equivalent to Rajyoga. These are:

1. When owners of the first, ninth and fifth houses are conjunct.

2. When owners of the second, sixth and tenth houses are conjunct.

3. When owners of the third, seventh and eleventh are conjunct.

4. When owners of the fourth, eighth and twelfth are conjunct.

Defining the good effects created by such yogas, Upaddhya explains that (i) when owners of the first, ninth and fifth are conjunct, such a yoga bestows on the native great respect in society, makes him/her a great leader, great scientist or highly devoted person. (ii) When owners of the second, sixth and tenth are conjunct in a chart, the yoga benefits the native living in foreign lands and makes him/her very rich. The native may also become a great businessman. Such a native is highly respected by the government. (iii) When owners of the third, seventh and eleventh are conjunct, such a yoga bestows great courage to help the native earn his/her wealth and, in spite of ups and downs, the native tends to be successful in life. (iv) The conjuncts of the fourth, eighth and twelfth houses do not provide the native any sort of happiness (*sukh*) in life. He/she often cultivates bad thoughts and consequently moves in the wrong direction. The native is often lethargic, unique in behaviour, and has a tendency to commit crimes.

Besides the above, even if the owners of any two houses, mainly of *trikonas* and *kendras,* such as the first, fourth, seventh, ninth, tenth, are conjunct in any of these houses, the native will enjoy Rajyoga. It will provide him/her great happiness, wealth, fame and help the native perform well.

Vipreet Rajyoga

So far we have not discussed much about the 6th, 8th and 12th houses, which are also very important in a chart and may form beneficial yogas that are at par with Rajyogas. Let us discuss briefly what *Vipreet Rajyoga* is.

1. If owners of the 6th, 8th or 12th sit in these houses, they form *Vipreet Rajyoga* and provide benefits to the native, which are almost equal to that of Rajyogas.

2. If owners of these houses sit in either of these houses, they form *Vipreet Rajyogas.* For example, if Virgo is rising in a chart the owner of the 8th house is Mars. In case Mars is sitting in the 12th house, it forms *Vipreet Rajyoga*, providing the native money, position, promotional benefits and lucrative foreign travel.

We can refer to a chart denoting all the aforesaid benefits to the native when Mars *dasha* was operating in his chart. He was around 48 years old at that time. Briefly, the chart belongs to a native born on 1 January around 12.30 a.m., Sunday in 1933. Virgo is rising in the chart and Mars and Ketu are sitting in the 12th house. During the said *dasha* in his life, the native was working abroad. Suddenly, he was promoted in his job and travelled around half the world. In appreciation of his service over nine years, all his travelling expenses were borne by the institution. When Ketu *dasha* was operating, the native received benefits like those he had enjoyed during his 48th year, when Mars *dasha* was operating. Mars forms *Vipreet Rajyoga, and* being the owner of the 8[th,] sitting in the 12th house, helped him get the benefits.

3. If a planet owns either of two houses from the 6th, 8th or 12th and sits in one of them, or if two planets belonging to these houses sit in any of these houses, *Vipreet Rajyoga* is formed. Such a yoga will provide the native every kind of happiness (*sukh*), various sorts of gains, and help the native make friends with great and influential people.

Let us now examine a number of charts to highlight Rajyogas referred to above, and other yogas. The reader must go through each chart very carefully and try to identify the yogas, conjuncts or aspects of the planet and verify what he/she has learnt so far in relation to examining a chart.

Kalsarpa Yoga

It is also very important to indicate *Kalsarpa Yoga* in brief, which has a very important bearing on a native's chart. This yoga is formed when all the planets are placed between Rahu and Ketu. Most astrologers reckon this as a bad yoga but Ramesh Upaddhya considers it to be an unusual yoga, which can also bestow good results. The yoga can make the native ambitious, courageous and hard working and may make him/her famous too. The results of this yoga are experienced after 38 years. The native will enjoy the above results only if the owner of the tenth is conjunct with Rahu, or if Rahu is placed in the third or fifth and makes *Kalsarpa Yoga*.

Case Study One

Before reaching any conclusions about the future of an individual, it is absolutely imperative that the position and strength of ascendant must be studied carefully. Much depends on it to boost an individual's future or luck. It can easily be judged by concrete examples. The following chart belongs to a 54-year-old surgeon employed by a state government in India for the last 26 years. He was born in Delhi on 27 May 1950. The position of the ascendant, and the effect of the aspects of the Sun, Jupiter, Saturn, Mars and other planets on the ascendant and other houses, which make the houses vulnerable to good and bad effects, are presented here.

Birth Chart of Native Born on 27 May 1950

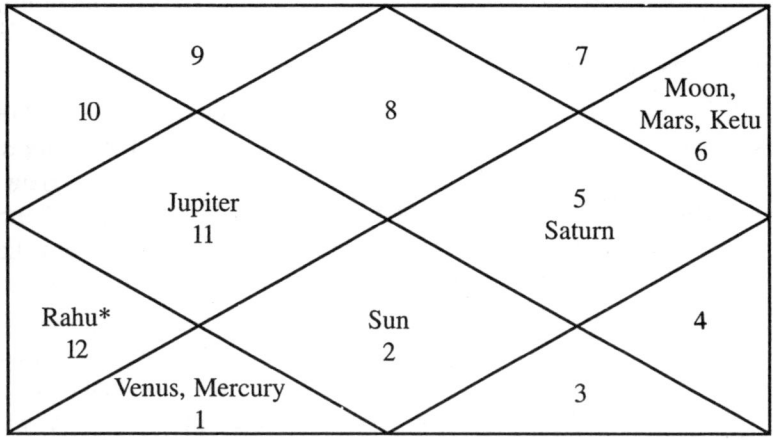

* **Note:** *Rahu & Ketu are considered as the Moon's nodes in Western astrology. They influence the native according to their placement in a house, as well as according to the planet in whose sign they appear in a chart.*

1. Strength of Ascendant

Mars the owner of the ascendant is sitting in the eleventh house and is conjunct with the Moon. Since the eleventh house relates to sudden financial benefits, as far as money is concerned, the native's position should be very bright. Besides, the owner of the ninth house, the Moon is also sitting with it. It makes a kind of Rajyoga (enjoying benefits like a Raja or ruler). The owner of the ascendant and the owner of the ninth house being in conjunction is highly beneficial to the native. It boosts his financial status and suggests that the native will never be short of money. Ketu's conjunction with the other two planets also adds to his finances, except that the means of earnings may be different at times.

But Ketu adds another element. It provides benefits according to Mars but, being malefic, adds a new dimension to the native's personality — some kind of bad effect in the conduct, making him either stubborn or sharp-tongued, or both, and it may also affect his thought process adversely by not permitting him to see things very clearly at times. In any case, the placement of the owner of the ascendant (Mars) in the eleventh house is highly beneficial, especially as the ascendant is in conjunction with the owner of the ninth house (Moon), which provides him good luck. Thus, the ascendant becomes very powerful and beneficial.

Besides, it is primarily on account of Mars that the native chose the medical profession. He is a surgeon because the owner of the tenth house, the Sun, has its full aspect on the ascendant. Keeping all that in view, when we assess the strength of the ascendant, we find it is very powerful. It provides the native with the qualities of determination, persistence, and ability to be a good surgeon, as the owner of the tenth house (Sun) has its aspect on the ascendant. The Sun is in Taurus, which is a sign ruled by Venus. It cultivates certain artistic qualities, such as love for music, arts and, consequently, refinement in surgery. Since the ascendant (here, the first house) is also in conjunction with the Sun on account of having its (Sun's) aspect on it, its strength has doubled.

There is one more factor that needs the reader's attention— the ascendant Mars, though not quite benefic, is conjunct with a great benefic, the Moon. The Moon and Mars are also permanent friends, according to tradition. Therefore, it often influences the native's way of thinking positively.

2. Ninth and Eleventh Houses
Let's now examine the ninth and eleventh houses in the chart of the surgeon. The ninth house is related to travel and foreign tours. Since its owner (Moon) is in the eleventh house and is placed with the owner of the ascendant (Mars), the native got a chance to travel to Iran and earned quite a lot of money in three years. This helped him complete some very important personal projects, such as building a big house and helping his children get good education. In fact, the conjunct of Mars and Moon is financially very beneficial and more helpful when this combination occurs in the eleventh house. Thus both, the ninth and eleventh houses are extremely powerful in the chart.

However, Ketu is also placed in the eleventh house, which may have a slightly negative impact on the house in some way. We have already indicated its negative effects on the native's behaviour and manner of earnings on account of Ketu's influence.

3. Tenth House

Let's examine the tenth house of the native very carefully. Saturn is sitting in the tenth house in Leo and is the owner of the third and fourth houses. In fact, Saturn is transiting in its enemy's sign (Leo). As a result, it may not provide much benefit to the native as far as his job is concerned. It has resulted in frequent transfers against his desire and tiresome efforts to sort out matters of this kind. But according to tradition, any planet in the tenth house should be beneficial. As such, the native's brothers' position is very strong. Not only that, he has four brothers, all of whom are highly educated and very well placed. Besides, he knows many influential people occupying high positions in society. This has happened because the owner of the third house Saturn is sitting in the tenth.

4. The Aspects

Now let's examine the aspects by the planets. The rule is that Saturn has aspects on the third, seventh and tenth houses from its position. In view of that, Saturn sitting in the tenth house has it aspects on the twelfth, fourth and seventh houses. Its aspect on the twelfth house has made the native spend a lot of money for one reason or another. For instance, the prolonged ailment of his wife, who died of cancer in 1997–98. Its aspect on the fourth house is highly beneficial as it is Saturn's own house. It helped him build a big and comfortable house. But its aspect on the seventh house has been detrimental, as it has resulted in the demise of his wife. It also eclipsed the Sun's positive influence by its aspect on it, as Saturn is the natural enemy of the Sun.

Besides, the tenth house has something more in store. The owner of the tenth house, the Sun, is sitting in the tenth house from its ownership. That boosts the power of the tenth house. Again, the sign Leo is rising in the tenth house, which has Jupiter's aspect on it. All these influences and aspects have ultimately extended the power of the tenth house, although Saturn's aspect on the owner of the tenth house (Sun) is not good. Besides, the Sun also has its aspects on the ascendant, which belongs to its friend, Mars. It has further boosted the ascendant's power. Consequently, the native has a good reputation as a surgeon amongst friends and patients. As a doctor he is highly valued and given due respect by his seniors and authorities.

Let us now move on to another chart for analysis.

The reader should bear in mind that, according to tradition, the placement of any benefic planet in the ascendant or in the fifth, ninth, tenth or eleventh houses, adds to the strength of that planet and the house as well.

Case Study Two

In the previous case study we concentrated on examining the ascendant, ninth, tenth and eleventh houses. While presenting the second case study, however we shall examine not only those houses, but also include two more, the fourth and seventh houses, because there is something special about them that we'd like to reveal.

On several occasions, we have referred to the chart of the native born in Jodhpur, Rajasthan, on 3 March 1962. He has a post-graduate degree in engineering and has been living in the United States for the last 20 years. We provide his complete chart at this juncture, and examine the conjuncts and aspects of the planets on various houses and highlight the strength of the ascendant.

Birth Chart of Native Born on 3 March 1962

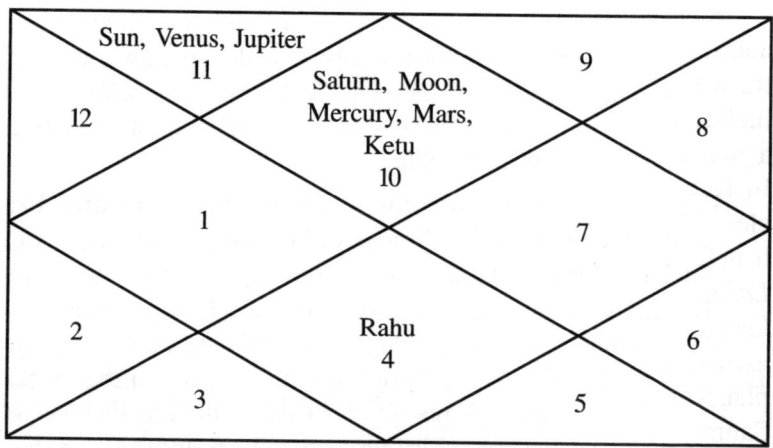

1. Strength of Ascendant and Aspects

As Capricorn is rising at the ascendant and its owner Saturn is sitting in it, basically the ascendant has become very strong. It has bestowed on the native great practical ability. It has also provided him with terrific powers of concentration and dedication towards work. He chose engineering because exalted Mars and strong Saturn are sitting at the ascendant. The native is endowed with creative talents and practicality on account of Capricorn rising at the ascendant and Mercury sitting in it. Mercury being the owner of the ninth house is conjunct with Mars and Saturn, the owners of the fourth, eleventh, first and second houses respectively.

Besides, because Ketu is sitting with Mars and Saturn in the ascendant, it endows the native with great zeal and high spirits with which he/she performs his/her professional work. The native has got *ruchak yoga*, which is one of the *panchmahapurush yoga*. This yoga is formed when Mars is in an exalted position at the ascendant, which makes the native highly assertive and professionally well equipped. One more dimension, great power of imagination, has been added to the native's personality by the placement of the Moon along with Mars and Saturn in the ascendant. All the four planets sitting in the first house, along with Ketu, have provided great strength to the ascendant, sturdy health, dashing gait, fascinating personality, bestowing on the native high ability to concentrate and to discover answers to the most difficult questions relating to his profession.

Since Mars and Saturn are owners of the fourth, eleventh, first and second houses respectively, and are conjunct at the ascendant, the native enjoys benefits of property and a great rise in career till his/her 40th birthday. The native also possesses the ability to earn a great deal of money and wealth from hard work and intelligence. In fact, the conjunct of the owners of the second (wealth) and eleventh (sudden gains) houses at the ascendant bestows a highly beneficial yoga relating to amassing great wealth, also known as *Laxmi Yoga*. According to Indian astrological traditions, Laxmi is known as the goddess of wealth. Thus, from every aspect, the ascendant is profusely strong as far as beneficial influences of the planets are concerned, except that the Moon is also conjunct with Saturn, which bestows melancholy moods at times on account of his mate and family matters.

2. Seventh House

But there are a few other things that need our atttention while examining the strength of the ascendant. In this particular chart the owner of the seventh house is playing quite an important role for the native. Although Ketu rising in Capricorn at the ascendant is likely to benefit the native with the same qualities that Saturn would give, it also curtails the ability of the native to take right decisions at times, as its placement in the ascendant cannot be totally considered beneficial. Besides, it eclipses the Moon being conjunct with it (in *Lagna*) and afflicts the native's emotional life, causing him distress on account of the partner. Ketu not only eclipses the Moon, but also has direct influence on the seventh house, which is the house of the native's partner.

The seventh house of the native also has aspects from the exalted Mars and powerful Saturn. Though Mars is exalted in the ascendant, its aspect on the seventh house is of debilitated nature.* Saturn's aspect on the seventh house, which is not its friend's house, is also not quite beneficial. All this suggests that the seventh house of the native is badly afflicted on account of certain planets' aspects, as well as with the Moon being in conjunct with Ketu and Saturn. Placement of Rahu in the seventh house also mars the benefits of that house.

But the seventh house has a positive aspect too. The Moon being its owner has its full aspect on it and has been helping the native to continue the matrimonial relationship against great odds.

3. Ninth and Tenth Houses

The owner of the ninth house is also the owner of the sixth house. So it may bring ailments at times, especially colds, coughs, headaches and problems relating to nerves. But Mercury being the owner of the ninth house ensures good luck in terms of job offers, suggesting job changes and good communicational ability. The owner of the tenth house Venus is also the owner of the fifth house and is conjunct with the eighth and twelfth house owners, the Sun and Jupiter. It also predicts job changes and, at times, indecision about changing jobs. Since Jupiter and Venus are not friendly with each

---

* *Every planet from its exalted position (and sign) has its debilitated aspects on the opposite house.*

other (*see Table 4:4*), and are conjunct in the second house, it has a bearing on the native's job status, earnings and expenses.

The native is very ambitious on account of strong Mars and Saturn conjunct at the ascendant. But the owner of the tenth house, Venus, being conjunct with the owner of the twelfth, Jupiter (traditional enemy of Venus), has influenced the native's ambitions as his thought process relating to jobs and education is afflicted by it. Table 4:4 will provide a clear picture of planets' being friendly, not unfriendly, and inimical to each other and enlighten you in understanding the relationships between the planets to judge the strength of the houses.

Table 4:5

Planets' Friends & Enemies

Ruling Planet	Permanent Friends	Not Quite Unfriendly	Enemy
Mars	Jupiter, Moon, Sun	Saturn	
Venus	Mercury, Saturn	Sun	Jupiter
Mercury	Venus, Saturn	Sun	
Moon	Jupiter, Sun, Mars	Venus, Mercury	Saturn
Sun	Mars, Jupiter, Moon	Mercury, Venus	Saturn
Jupiter	Sun, Moon, Mars	Mercury	Venus
Saturn	Venus, Mercury	Jupiter, Mars	Sun

In fact, Jupiter, owner of the twelfth house (waste and expenditure) being conjunct with the owner of the tenth house, Venus, tends to develop the habit of extravagance both in terms of money and jobs. Since Venus is also the owner of the fifth house, Jupiter also tends to afflict that house, which relates to children and education. But Mercury sitting in the ascendant and Venus being conjunct with the Sun, have sliced down Jupiter's influence in that respect. However, it is still going to affect the native's educational career and relationship with children in some way and to some extent.

4. Fourth and Eleventh Houses

The native's fourth and eleventh houses are well placed, as its owner Mars is in exaltation and is conjunct with the strong ascendant, forming very powerful yoga (combinations). Exalted Mars at the ascendant is bestowing *Ruchak Yoga*. We have already stated the benefits of this kind of conjunct (Mars and Saturn) at the ascendant. It will always bestow good luck to the native in terms of owning valuable property, good conveyance (transport), and love from the family (mother and father). Keeping in view the placement of exalted Mars in the ascendant, the native should choose north-east directions to settle down in life, except that the impact of a strong ascendant, Saturn, will go on influencing the native's mind to stay in the south-west directions. But in view of the position of the owner of the tenth, Venus, he should choose (north) west direction, which is also suggested by Mars to a great extent. Such directions are considered from the native's permanent home in the US.

Case Study Three

We present another chart for reference. The native was born on 20 July 1964 at Udaipur, Rajasthan, and was around 39 years old when his chart was analysed. He has a post-graduate degree in English Literature and is employed by the Government of India as an IRS, serving as a very senior officer in the cadre. Besides analysing the first, fifth, eighth, ninth and tenth houses, a brief survey of the seventh and eleventh houses will also be made after presenting the chart. Let's first examine the strength of the (*Lagna*) ascendant and discover different benefic combinations (yogas), which helped the native reach a very high position in the Revenue Department in the Central Government at quite an early age.

Birth Chart of Native Born on 20 July 1964

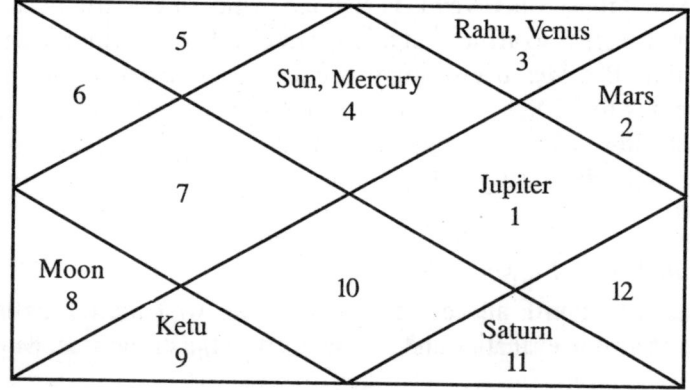

1. Strength of Ascendant

The ascendant Moon is placed in the fifth house in the sign Scorpio, which is its friend's sign. It's a beneficial placement of the ascendant, as it helps the native to be very thoughtful, imaginative and develops a poetic sense in him. Besides, he will always love reading and may write poems and other material occasionally. But as Moon is traditionally considered in debilitation in Scorpio, it also tends to cultivate some sort of ill thoughts, anger, brooding and the habit of grumbling in the native.

The placement of the Sun and Mercury is very helpful and provides great power to the ascendant. The Sun being the owner of the second house (wealth, family and speech), rising in Cancer in a friendly sign, provides all related benefits to the native. Besides, the Mercury and Sun conjunct at the ascendant endows the native with the ability of good planning, quick comprehension and seeking quick solutions to problems as well as having an edge in computing and calculations.

But Mercury being the owner of the third and twelfth houses is beneficial as well as not so beneficial. As far as its ownership of the third house is concerned, it makes the native very hard working and bestows the quality to take the initiative. But Mercury being the owner of the twelfth house (waste, expenditure, travel), the native also tends to spend a lot, especially on brothers and friends. Still, the Sun rising in the ascendant provides the native with a sense of dignity, respect as well as faith in religion.

2. Fifth House

Although we have referred to a few things about the fifth house while analysing the strength of the ascendant, the fifth house needs to be examined separately. Its owner Mars is sitting in the eleventh house, which benefits the native financially and indicates that he will certainly have some sort of benefit from children. Although the placement of the Moon in it indicates daughters but, as the house has a direct aspect from its owner, he should also be blessed with a son, most probably at the age of 41 and/or 43. The native tends to read a lot and enjoys the company of books. There are some chances of miscarriage, which should be taken care of. As the ascendant is sitting in the fifth house, it makes him imaginative, moody and at times doleful. It also tends to sharpen the tongue, invoking enmity and displeasure of friends. He should guard against this tendency.

Now let's examine the owner of the fifth house, which is sitting just opposite it in the eleventh house. It also suggests benefits from the father and the government. The children may earn good scholarships from their school and college. We observe a kind of triangle between the first, fifth and eleventh houses. Mutual aspects by the owners of the first and fifth houses (Moon and Mars) make *Saraswati Yoga*, which signifies great intellectual capability in the native.

3. Ninth and Tenth Houses

Tradition recognises that when the owner of the ninth sits in the tenth house, or if there is an exchange between the owners of ninth and tenth houses, it is considered *Rajyoga*, which simply means having benefits like a Raja. The native has this yoga in his chart. Jupiter the owner of the ninth is transiting in the tenth house, which is the house of its friend, Mars. Jupiter is supposed to be very strong in Aries, as it is a fiery sign. The native will enjoy great respect at work and will be liked by his superiors, but there will always be someone who will be displeased and backbite him. The native should guard against someone who seems very close but in reality may not be so.

We see a great beneficial placement of the owner of ninth sitting in the tenth, and the owner of the tenth is sitting in the eleventh. Thus, Mars and Jupiter are in total control of three very beneficial houses, the ninth (luck), tenth (job/work), and eleventh (sudden gains). This sort of placement of two very important planets in the native's chart has accelerated good luck, prestige, status, and financial benefits from the government.

4. Seventh and Eleventh Houses

If we examine these two houses and their owners separately, we find that these houses are not quite strong, as the owner of the eleventh, Venus, is sitting in the twelfth house (expenditure, waste, losses, etc.) Since Venus also rules the fourth house of the native, it mars the benefits of that house too. It predicts the native's mother's ill health and some kind loss of mobile and/or immobile property. Thus, the position of Venus is quite detrimental in the chart. It also suggests that the native's relationship with the partner may not always be very smooth. This is also further suggested by the Sun's aspect on the seventh house. We shall discuss the position of the seventh house and other houses when we examine the aspects from planets. If Mars were not in a very commanding position, the native's finances would always be in jeopardy.

5. The Aspects

The quality and status of this chart has been raised quite high by aspects of the planets. For example, the aspect of the owner of the ninth (Jupiter) on the fourth house has largely restored the bad effects created on account of Venus' placement in the twelfth, although all may not be restored. Besides, the ill effects created by the ascendant being in the debilitated sign in the fifth are much mitigated by the aspect of the owner of the fifth (Mars) on it. Mars may give an anger-ridden temperament, but may check the native from speaking unpleasant things or being secretive, which are suggested by the debilitated Moon. The conjunct of Mercury with the Sun in the first house has increased the imaginative ability and will power of the native to a large extent and mitigated the ill effects of the debilitated Moon.

The Moon's exalted aspect on the eleventh house has benefited the native with untold financial gains and reduced the ill effects of Venus' placement in the twelfth house. Above all, the aspect of Mars on the second, fifth and sixth houses has benefited the native in terms of finances, good memory and creative ability, and by reducing tension from criticism (enemies).

At this juncture, we would like to state the position and aspects of Saturn before winding up our discussion on this chart. Saturn's placement in the eighth house in its own sign gives a very long life (90 plus) to the native, except that he may have short periods of ailments in between. But its aspect on the second house has restricted the native's power of eloquence, although the Sun sitting in the first house restores it to some extent. The Sun's aspect on the seventh house, which is the house of its enemy (Saturn), cannot be considered good. It suggests some kind of ill will and difference of opinion between him and the partner, disrupting peace and incurring displeasure at times.

Aspects from benefic planets on a house or a planet, or on both, add to the strength of that house.

Case Study Four

We present the case of a senior government employee in the Police Department and involved with the enforcement of law and order. The native was born on 9 August 1951, near Gwalior, M.P. He was around 52 years when this analysis was done. He has travelled a lot within the country. He is a science post-graduate and has a couple of children, who are fairly well educated and employed in the private sector in different states in the country.

Like the other three cases, once again, let us examine the first, fifth, seventh, ninth, tenth and eleventh houses for reference. Before we draw the native's chart (*kundali*), we wish to state that most human qualities, as well as a successful career, depend largely on the strength of the ascendant. No individual can command the respect and goodwill of others if the ascendant is weak in his/her chart.

Birth Chart of Native Born on 9 August 1951

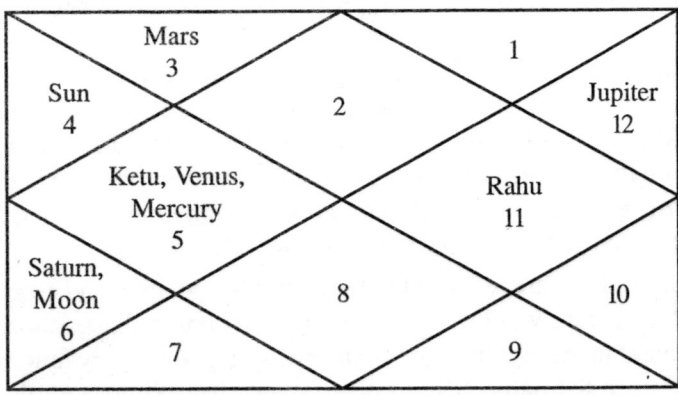

1. Strength of Ascendant

The ascendant, Venus, is conjunct with its permanent friend, Mercury, and is sitting in the fourth house, which is related to family, mother and general happiness of the native. As such its placement is quite good, but it is also conjunct with Ketu, which tends to infuse anger and a tendency to criticise and grumble. Since Venus is the owner of the first and sixth houses, it tends to give some kind of mental agony for no real reason. A tendency of apprehension is also possible by the Moon conjunct with Saturn in the fifth house.

But the ill effect created by the conjunct of Saturn and Moon is mitigated, as Jupiter has its aspect on the Moon. Mercury and Venus transiting in Leo are one sign before being exalted and debilitated respectively. Both are important planets for the native as Venus is the owner of the ascendant and Mercury is the owner of the fifth house. So, the native is unpredictable at times, which is in keeping with his job. However, Ketu in a fiery sign infuses the native with zeal and agility, which are good qualities anyway and also helpful to the native's work in a particular field. Thus, the overall position and strength of the ascendant is quite unpredictable and unusual.

2. Fourth House

The owner of the fourth, the Sun is placed in the third house making the position of the native's brothers very strong. He has six brothers and sisters, with more than half being males. All of them are married, fruitfully employed and nicely settled in life. All have separate houses, personal transport, some having very expensive cars too. Thus, the Sun's rising in the third house being its friend's house has been very lucky for the native. The native has a good number of well-placed and helpful friends too. Sitting in the third house, the Sun has also made him very hard working, persistent and dutiful. It has helped him a lot in his job. So, the fourth house is very strong and its owner sitting in the third has influenced the third a lot. The owner of the third, however, is conjunct with Saturn and is not as strong as the Sun.

3. Fifth, Ninth and Tenth Houses

It is important to examine these houses simultaneously, as it will provide a clearer picture about the native's overall progress. The owner of the ninth and tenth, Saturn is sitting in the fifth house, which is the house of education, intellect, children, production, and also has a bearing on the native's thinking process. Transiting in Virgo in the fifth house, Saturn provides the quality of quick thinking and agility in temperament. Besides, Saturn in Virgo is transiting in its permanent friend's house. Traditionally it is considered

149

to be exalted in the next sign. So, Saturn is in a very strong position and, thus, the ninth and the tenth houses of the native are very strong and helpful in his progress.

The owner of the fifth, Mercury, sitting in the fourth house in Leo is also about to be exalted. Thus, the fifth house is very strong in the chart. The mere placement of the Moon in the fifth house causes some kind of malice in the thought process of the native, and affects his relationship with brothers and sisters to some extent. But it makes the native quite imaginative and farsighted as well as secretive, which are useful qualities for his job. When we discuss the effects of planets' aspects on the houses, we will unfold the strength of these houses.

4. The Aspects

The total strength of the above chart lies with aspects of the planets on the houses and planets. The aspect of the owner of the eleventh (Jupiter) on the fifth house and Saturn (the owner of the ninth and tenth) has elevated the strength of the fifth, ninth and tenth houses. It has benefited the native by providing a logical bent of mind, and reduced the ill effects of the Moon and Saturn conjunct. It strengthens the position of children too. We also clearly see a promise of a higher position in his career, when he reaches his fifty-sixth and fifty-seventh years. There is something unusual in this chart as far as the aspects of Mars and Saturn are concerned. Both these planets have aspects on each other. Saturn is sitting in the fourth house from Mars and Mars is sitting in the tenth house from Saturn, having full aspect on each other.

Besides, Mars' look (aspect) on the ninth house (luck) is of exalted nature. Mars exalts in Capricorn. Thus, Mars' aspect has been very lucky for the native, providing him the right kind of job. Besides, Saturn, the owner of the ninth house also has its aspect on the ninth house. Therefore, on account of Mars, Saturn and also Jupiter, both houses, the ninth and tenth, have gratified. The eleventh house is good in itself as its owner Jupiter is sitting in it and has aspects from Saturn, the owner of the ninth and tenth.

The strength of the tenth house has further been enlarged on account of Rahu sitting in it. As Rahu is transiting in Saturn's sign Aquarius, it is bound to give quite positive results most of the time, especially when it transits in Aquarius. It enables the native to be successful in his projects, and helps in getting commendations from his department. The native will have good support from seniors at home and at work. On some occasions he may encounter resistance on account of his own temperament being coloured by Rahu and Ketu, as both have some kind of conjunct on the native's weak ascendant. At this point, a brief examination of the seventh house is necessary. Both the seventh house and the owner of the seventh, Mars, have Saturn's malefic aspects. As such, the seventh house has been adversely affected, except that Jupiter, a permanent benefic, has its aspect on it. It has helped in sustaining the relationship with the partner and proved to be a boon in life.

Remember that unless the owner of the ascendant is strong and has aspects from benefic planets on it and on the ascendant as well, the native will not possess a positive bent of mind.

Case Study Five

The following is the chart of a Professor of Physics, who works in a privately owned reputed college in Rajasthan. He has four brothers who are very well placed in life. The native has three sons, who have good higher education abroad and were in the process of getting settled in life when this analysis was made. His wife is also highly educated and they both have been living quite a satisfactory life for almost three decades. Let us examine the strength of the ascendant first, before examining other important houses.

Birth Chart of Native Born on 6 November 1945

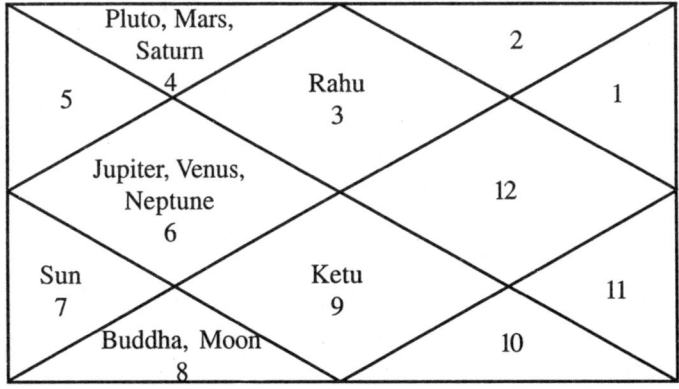

1. Strength of Ascendant and the Fourth house

The native's ascendant is transiting the sixth house, which is quite an unusual placement. Though the ascendant Mercury is sitting in the sixth house, traditionally its own house, it is not a very happy placement. The sixth house relates to enemies, sickness, opposition, criticism, etc. Since the ascendant is in the sixth and is transiting in Mars' sign, Scorpio, it tends to bestow upon the native's temperament some kind of anguish and anger, which may be reflected from time to time in his behaviour. This affects his thought process regularly. Mercury is also conjunct with the debilitated Moon, the owner of the second house that relates to speech, hard-earned money, and family, etc. The Moon's placement in the sixth house cannot be considered a very hopeful placement, as it further affects the native's style of speech, making him often talk quite bluntly, which can be unpleasant for others.

However, both Mercury and the Moon are beneficial planets. Their conjunct can, at times, bestow some sort of benevolent and kind disposition. The placement of Rahu in Gemini (owned by Mercury) in the ascendant bestows literary taste and hunger for knowledge. It also tends to develop certain unpleasant food habits as Rahu is transiting the ascendant. The Jupiter and Venus conjunct in the fourth house has also dampened the native's thought process (as far as action is concerned) to some extent, although both have a direct aspect on the tenth house. Mercury being the owner of the ascendant and the fourth houses, and sitting in the sixth, has not helped the native construct his own house for a long time. Venus and Jupiter conjunct in the fourth house has further added to this delay, denying that sort of benefit for a long time.

It appears likely that the native may start constructing his own house on completing his sixtieth year. Rahu may also bestow good effects on the native at 60. In view of all this, it can be concluded that as far as the overall position and strength of the ascendant and the fourth house is concerned, it can be taken to be mixed. At times the native feels too strong within but on other occasions he becomes less agile, resulting in disappointments.

Jupiter and Venus conjunct in a house diminish the strength of the house where the conjunct occurs and also adversely affect the houses they own.

2. Third and Fifth Houses

The Sun, owner of the third house, is transiting the fifth house in its debilitated sign. But being the traditional owner of the fifth house, the Sun bestows intelligence and scientific temperament on the native. Besides, his earnings have always been through mental faculties, which is obvious from the Sun's aspect on the eleventh house (the house of gains). The native's mind should be very fertile in getting benefits through different sources and activities, involving selling, buying or investments. Friends and brothers should also be the source of benefits in some way. But the placement of a weak Venus (owner of the fifth house) in conjunction with Jupiter (its permanent enemy) may affect his relations with his children.

We can also infer that his educational career must have been influenced adversely in some way. Throughout his life, he may have indulged in two different kinds of ideas (while taking decisions). This may have kept him off the right track in life. Although he is far more intelligent than most people, this indecisiveness on occasions when a quick decision was earnestly needed has been the story of the native's life. This is why things have not worked in his favour. Thus, the overall strength of the third and fifth houses will have mixed effects on the native.

3. Ninth, Tenth and Eleventh Houses

The owner of the ninth (Saturn) and owner of the eleventh (Mars) are conjunct in the second house, which is the house of earned wealth, speech, family, social life, and personal debts, etc. Though Mars and Saturn own the eleventh and ninth houses, they also control the sixth and eighth houses respectively. Their ownership of sixth (Mars) and eighth (Saturn) houses has lessened their positive qualities. So they are not able to provide as much benefit to the native as they should have. Though the native will earn a lot, somehow or the other his earnings will be wasted and luck will not assist him as much as it should. When we examine the tenth house, we find that Jupiter, its owner, is sitting in the fourth, which is just opposite the tenth house. Thus, it has its direct aspect on the tenth house, which gives a lot of strength to it.

Besides, Venus also looks at the tenth house (exalted look) giving it full strength. Although the aspects of Venus and Jupiter provide a lot of strength to the tenth, they also drag the native in two opposite directions. This means the native has either given up some good chances of jobs or foregone some good opportunities on account of his indecision. Still, he should never suffer from want of a job or assignment even after retirement, though the job may or may not be to his liking. Both Mars and Saturn sitting in the second house have influenced the native's way of speech, which sometimes affects relations with those close to him. Rahu also affects his temperament and makes him act impulsively, although Gemini rising in the ascendant makes him quite prudent, imaginative and witty. The native needs to be more prudent in his speech and is required to say only what is most needed. It would help to keep good relationships with dear ones too.

4. Seventh House

A brief examination of the seventh house reveals that the partner should be quite adjusting as its owner Jupiter (highly benefic) is sitting in the tenth from the seventh. Besides, Jupiter being the owner of the tenth is also assisting the native in some way, in performing duties and by occasionally working and bringing some financial assistance to the family. But as Jupiter and Venus (permanent enemies) are conjunct in the fourth, it seems difficult to be united on a mental level, unless one of the two yields. Both need to exercise some restraint over their temperament, especially during crucial moments. Thus, although the overall strength of the seventh house is in plus it is definitely not quite wholesome.

5. The Aspects

Mars, Saturn, Venus, Sun and Jupiter have their aspects on different houses in the chart, and occasionally benefit the native. Mars' aspect on the fifth and ninth houses is quite beneficial. Its aspect on the Sun (fifth house) tends to provide a sharp and analytical thought process (mind), and its aspect on Aquarius (ninth house) boosts luck. Saturn's aspect on the third house (brothers and friends) is not beneficial, as it is the enemy's house. It causes disruption in relations with friends and brothers. If Mars were not looking at the Sun, such relations would end for good, but the owner of the third (the Sun) has Mars' aspect on it. It has altered Saturn's bad influence considerably. Saturn is also looking at the eleventh house (financial gains). Occasional gains from forest, land and activities like brokership could provide him some benefits. Both Jupiter and Venus have aspects on the tenth house.

Though these planets drag the native in opposite directions, they have a good impact on the house. Jupiter is the owner of the tenth house (Pisces rising) and Venus has its exalted aspect on it. So these aspects are good in their own way. Thus overall assessment of the chart is quite positive. The native has benefited from the planets 60 to 70 per cent of the time. To take more benefits from them he is required to wear a gold ring, with a 4½ carat *panna*, which would give him better control on his speech and ignite good vision while taking decisions.

Case Study Six

The following chart belongs to a Professor who worked at the NCERT, New Delhi for over 20 years and retired around ten years ago. During the years he worked for the NCERT, he occupied important positions, being involved with activities of paramount importance, both within the country and internationally. After retirement, he has been busy in organising international workshops and seminars, and writing and editing books of invaluable nature. The native has two daughters who are married and well settled. He was born in Uttar Pradesh on 19 October 1930. Let us examine his chart starting first with the analysis of the ascendant.

Birth Chart of Native Born on 19 October 1930

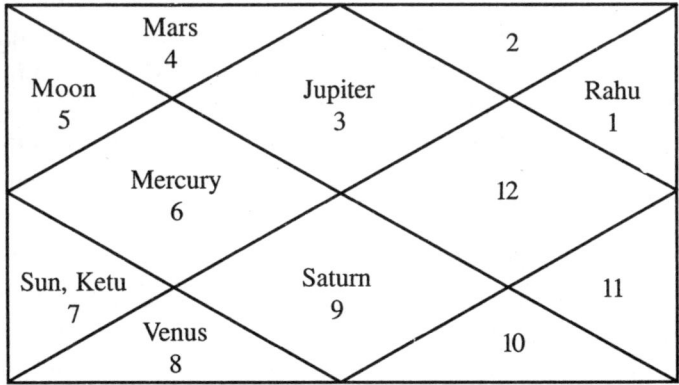

1. Strength of Ascendant

The owner of the ascendant Mercury is transiting in Virgo in the fourth house in its exalted sign. The ascendant is extremely strong from the very outset, making the native intellectually rich and helping him be in vigorous moods most of the time. It has also provided him a highly practical and constructive outlook. It is on account of the exalted Mercury, also the owner of the ascendant, that the native has been greatly interested in intellectual work. Besides, his confidence level in life should have always been very great, bestowing upon him great nervous energy most of the time. It is expected that the native should have been enormously keen to be fully occupied with work in life. On account of his great practical ability, he must have been busy with intellectual work.

Since Mercury has occupied the fourth house, the native should have more security from his mother (than the father), who would have extended patronage to him for quite a long time. As Mercury is exalted in the fourth house, the native tends to possess a lot of property, with the advantage of having servants and of living in good houses from an early age. Even later on, he must have lived in his own or other's houses with all comforts. When we examine the rising sign Gemini, we come to the conclusion that it has provided the native the ability to use a tremendous amount of energy on thinking. The native's mind would have seldom stopped working, even when he was asleep. But when the sign Gemini rises at the ascendant, it also provides the native something more.

Though the native is extremely charming, and accommodating, he can be unbelievably contrary when it suits him. Such a native should have great ideas, moments of great insight and great ability to inspire others. As Mercury is the ruling planet, it can help the native be a genius and great thinker. In view of all this, the native's ascendant is extremely strong. We will discuss a few other things about the ascendant's strength, when we discuss the planets' aspects on the ascendant and its owner.

2. Third and Fifth Houses

When we examine the third and fifth houses, we find that the owner of the third, the Sun, is sitting in the fifth in its debilitation sign. The Sun is also conjunct with Ketu, which is not a very healthy combination. It discloses that the native may not have very

156

good relations with his brothers and father. At times, it would have also affected his relations with friends. But the impact (aspect) of Mars on the Sun helps in reducing the ill effects of Ketu (and Rahu) to a certain extent. The native should have either two brothers and two sisters or only sisters, as brothers would have died when the native was still very young. As the Moon is sitting in the third house, the native should have better relations with his sisters than brothers.

Likewise, his friendship with women should have been more lasting and beneficial. If the Sun were not conjunct with Ketu, the native would have possessed a much better thought process and produced literature of far greater repute. Still the Sun will help him a lot in this respect, more so as Jupiter looks at it sitting in the ascendant. It is also worthwhile to examine the sixth house with the fifth, as the owner of the fifth, Venus, is sitting in the sixth house, which is the house of an enemy and critical outlook. At times, the native may have created enemies on account of his very critical reflections, both orally and in writing. As Venus is also the owner of the twelfth house and is sitting in the sixth house, it has helped the native check his expenses, making him somewhat of a miser. But the native would have always looked upon such habits as wise.

3. Seventh House

It is imperative to examine the seventh house of the native as it unfolds many matters relating to his happiness and progress. The owner of the seventh house, Jupiter, is transiting the first house (ascendant) in the native's chart. Besides, Jupiter has its full aspect on the seventh house. As such, he should have great happiness and comfort from his partner. But Saturn is also sitting in the seventh house. In fact, Saturn's transit in Sagittarius in the seventh house is not beneficial to the native as it provides unhappiness, poor relations and low adjustment with the partner. Whenever Saturn has had its aspects on Jupiter during its transits, and on the seventh house during its 30-year cycle, the relations must have reached its lowest ebbs (at least thrice for seven and half years in each cycle).

Indeed, close examination of the chart reveals an early marriage. The marriage could possibly take place when the native is either in his 19th, 21st or 23rd year. But soon after taking up a job at 24 or 25, he will have had extramarital relations. Such relations will have

157

continued till he was 58 years, or maybe even later. This can also be one reason for his poor relations with the partner. But life is expected to be normal with the partner until he is 79. After that there may be a sudden break in the relations.

4. Ninth, Tenth and Eleventh Houses

It is very important to examine these three important houses, which have contributed to the native's progress and affluence. The owner of the ninth, Saturn, is sitting in the seventh (eleventh from the ninth) in the chart and has its full aspect on it (ninth) from there. The owner of the tenth, Jupiter, is sitting in the ascendant and has its aspect on the ninth house. Thus, both the owners of the ninth and tenth have their full aspects on the ninth house, which bestows great luck on the native. Tradition reckons such aspects as Rajyogas. Such aspects have also benefited the native to travel to foreign countries. The native will have chances of travelling abroad during his 74th and 75th years. The owner of the eleventh house (sudden gains) Mars, is sitting in the second house (earned wealth) in a debilitated sign. It helped the native earn wealth (good money) from hard work. From time to time, it also provided opportunities and benefits of this kind from other sources too. In fact, if Mars were not in debilitation sign, it was almost Laxmi Yoga, which simply means amassing great wealth. Still, the native should never suffer from lack of sufficient wealth and position.

5. The Aspects

When we analyse the aspects of the planets on the houses we find that Saturn's aspects on the lagna (ascendant) and Mercury (owner of the ascendant) make the native tactful. He is prudent and cannot be easily fooled. It is on account of his unpredictable temperament (Gemini rising at the ascendant) and certain unusual food habits (created by Mars sitting in a debilitation sign) that the native has lost certain benefits in life. On account of Saturn's aspect on the Gemini ascendant and Jupiter, the native has been losing opportunities that have come to him due to his position, talent, intellectual ability and reputation. We have already discussed the aspects of Saturn and Jupiter on the ninth and tenth houses, which have proved beneficial for the native in terms of position, money, and authority etc. The aspect of Mars on the Sun should have benefited the native with at least one son, although it also tends to inflict miscarriages during 29th, 33rd and 37th years. But it is quite likely that the native will have one son, either through adoption or in some other way. As Jupiter has its aspect on the Sun and the Sun has its exalted aspect on the eleventh house, the native will have benefits from his daughters and also perhaps from the son.

The reader should, therefore, keep in mind that the aspects from friendly and unfriendly planets bestow good and bad results respectively.

Case Study Seven

We present the chart of Swami Ram Tirth, whose erratic and amoral activities in early life could never have indicated the promise of a highly religious and devoted life in future. He was born in Gujranwala, Punjab around 1902. Most of his activities are not a secret to us now. He started his career vaguely, spending every moment of adulthood in the company of unpleasant, anti-social people. Although we don't have the exact year of his birth, as his *kundali* was noted down from a book, we presume it to be around 1902. An analysis of Swami Ram Tirth's chart clearly confirms that it is on account of good aspects on his ascendant that he finally chose a higher mission in life. He possessed full faith in God and belief in His kindness, and finally died an ascetic. Much before his death, he devoted his life to the good of the people. Let us analyse his chart, especially the ascendant, which was mainly instrumental in bringing a change in his life's mission.

Chart of Swami Ram Tirth Born on 22 Oct.

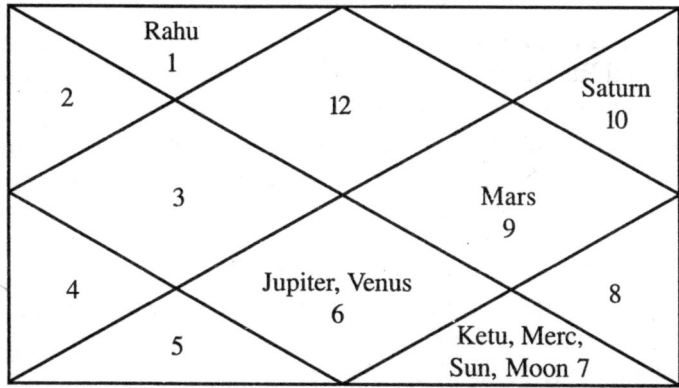

1. Strength of Ascendant and the Aspects

As Pisces is rising in the ascendant, it is obvious that the native will tend to drag his life in two different directions. When Pisces rises in a person's chart, both negative and positive qualities can emerge. The native will often be looking to the negative and positive sides of life. He will be critical of his own self and others. Perhaps this quality ultimately converted Ram Tirth into a God-loving person. Let us examine the chart carefully and try to discover the strength of the ascendant, which ultimately seemed to have helped him follow the right track in life.

The owner of the ascendant Jupiter is sitting in the seventh house, opposite the ascendant. This indicates the native will possess a tendency to follow the opposite sex, which means indulging in unwanted activities. As Venus is conjunct with Jupiter (ascendant), its permanent enemy, it influenced the ascendant adversely. Besides, such a combination (conjunct) in the seventh house leads to an unpredictable life as far as the native's relationship with women is concerned. Hence, Ram Tirth spent his early life in this manner.

But the ascendant (Pisces) has aspects from four planets of a different nature. We have already stated that planets' aspects on the houses provides them with many negative and positive qualities. Mars' aspect on the ascendant from the tenth house is obviously good, as it is the friend's house. Saturn also has its aspect on the ascendant, which tends to make the native contemplative and thoughtful. Venus' aspect on the ascendant is of exalted nature, which provides him with extraordinary wealth of knowledge and artistic qualities, including love for music. Finally, Jupiter's aspect on its own house restores all kinds of good thinking in the native.

So, it is mainly on account of excellent aspects on the ascendant of Swami Ram Tirth that he finally led a highly religious life. The only reason for his not adhering to a normal, moral life in the beginning is a debilitated Venus conjunct with Jupiter in the seventh house. Thus, the ascendant has become extremely strong on account of the aspects of various planets on it.

2. Conjunct of Four Planets

Tradition confirms that a combination of four, or more than four, planets in a house leads one to follow an ascetic life ultimately. Four planets (including Ketu) are conjunct in Swami Ram Tirth's *kundali*, which tends to push him towards a far more pragmatic and purposeful life. Though Ketu is considered a shadow planet, it tends to provide the qualities of the sign in which it is transiting. Therefore, Ketu is likely to provide the native with the excellence that Venus would have bestowed on him. Thus, Mercury conjunct with Ketu, the Sun and Moon provided him with ascetic qualities.

As Swamiji is not alive today, his inner self cannot be revealed and verified, but when we examine the rising sign (Pisces) in his chart, we can conclude that he must have been a great critic of his own activities. Such an attitude must have led him to relinquish his wasteful life, and would have filled him with great remorse and repentance. Besides, the Sun rising in Libra provides a balance in emotions. His early career being spent in matters relating to amoral and unsociable activities needed to be balanced on account of the Sun rising in Libra. The Moon's influence (in Libra) gave him the elements of bravery and kindness and also sympathy for people. It certainly requires great fortitude to relinquish a lustful life. Again, Mercury transiting in Libra provided him with compassion and consideration for people, making him feel relaxed with them. Ketu provided him with the qualities of appreciation, possessing extremely tender and kind feelings for others. Such excellence was likely to bestow great social qualities, which ultimately benefited him.

In fact, the eighth house is a kind of house that reflects many unusual characteristics in comparison to the other houses of the chart. It is the only house that indicates conditions and circumstances that can bring death to the native. It can indicate the time of accident(s), unusual events leading to death-like situations, serious illness, travels, benefits of hidden wealth, longevity and shortness of life and the *native's interest in spiritual matters can also be predicted by the position and strength of this house.* Thus, the conjunct of the four planets in the eighth house, including a full (exalted) aspect of Saturn on it, gave Swamiji quite a long life, despite the fact that he did not care much for his health in the beginning.

3. Other Yogas
Tradition suggests that if Saturn transits in Capricorn in a chart, it is quite likely that the native may attain *moksha* (salvation) in life. It is really a matter of further research what different effects Saturn transiting in Capricorn in various houses can provide. But

Saturn in Capricorn in the eleventh house has its full aspect on the ascendant, and has its exalted aspect on the eighth house, which is also the house (besides death and accidents) relating to spiritual matters. Saturn's aspect on the ascendant makes one quite thoughtful, diplomatic and also inward looking. In Swamiji's chart, Saturn provides a kind of *sadhu yoga*, which involves relinquishing all sorts of household benefits and reckless physical involvement. I, therefore, conclude that Swami Ram Tirth, on account of various kinds of aspects on his ascendant and due to four planets' conjunct in the eighth house, was ultimately bound to lead an ascetic's life, irrespective of what he was in the early part of his life.

Therefore, it must be borne in mind that conjuncts formed in a chart add to the strength of the houses, bestowing benefits on the native. Besides, it is also obvious that aspects on the houses, especially on the ascendant, are highly meaningful.

Case Study Eight

We present the chart of an industrialist who, a couple of years ago, was enjoying a princely status and was extremely busy with his business. He possessed two big firms—one, an offset printing machine, with a tremendous turnover and financial benefits. The second one, a yarn industry in operation, but with many impediments. The changes in his fortunes started a couple of years ago, which is when the analysis of his chart was done. He was born in Shimla, north India. Currently he is settled in southern Rajasthan and has been struggling for survival in the business.

Chart of Native Born on 26 Sept. 1959

162

1. Strength of Ascendant and Tenth House

Mercury sitting at the ascendant and also as the owner of the tenth house has given great natural strength to the native. The owner of the ascendant Mercury is exalted. It has provided the native with highly intellectual qualities, mixed with courage, perseverance, and persistence to face difficult situations. Mercury, the owner of the tenth and first houses, has diverted the native's attention towards the yarn and printing businesses, which are absolutely controlled by Mercury. Mars, the owner of the third house, has the added quality of persistence, which is highly useful in business. Except that Mars also owns the eighth house, which indicates some kind of damage or accident at eight, 20 and 32 years, Mars has made the native highly industrious. Rahu is almost in its exalted sign, which provides the native with a deep sense of understanding of matters not seen by the open eye. He can figure out matters gradually and is capable of finding solutions to his problems. Except that the Sun, the owner of the twelfth house, and sitting in the first house, the ascendant, is pretty strong. The Sun has provided him extravagance and an urge to spend when he does not need to spend. When good days operated the habit of extravagance and certain other temptations, especially food habits, have drawn the native to a direction that he would not have followed if the Sun were not sitting in the ascendant. Still the Sun in Virgo makes him God-fearing, possessing a decent disposition, but occasionally temperamental.

The tenth has become stronger, as the owner of the eleventh house is sitting in it. Though the owner of the eleventh house is in the twelfth house from it (eleventh), it is going to provide him financial benefits from work or business.

2. Seventh, Fifth and Fourth Houses

The owner of the fifth is sitting in the fourth, the owner of the fourth is sitting in the third, which is twelve houses from the signs. It has reduced the benefits of the fourth and fifth houses in terms of delay in constructing a house for him as well as getting the children settled sooner in life. However, the owner of the seventh house is sitting in the third house, which is the ninth house from the seventh. It has helped the native in terms of his married life, except that Ketu sitting in the seventh house is occasionally ill-bearing on the house, disturbing the family peace temporarily.

3. Ninth House

The ninth house is absolutely important. If its owner is well placed it will enhance the luck of the native but if it is placed in the sixth, eighth or twelfth house it is bound to reduce the quality of the house. Since the native's Venus, the owner of the ninth house, is sitting in the twelfth house, it has affected his luck adversely. Besides, Venus also controls the second house, which governs earned wealth and family matters. So, Venus has adversely affected both. The native's hard-earned wealth will have to wait until he is over 44 years old. Besides, Jupiter's transit in Leo at that age will increase the damage. As soon as he completes 45 years, circumstances will start favouring him as the owner of the tenth (46th year), Mercury, is sitting at the ascendant in its exalted sign. Jupiter's transits in Virgo, Libra, and Scorpio will be especially good for him. Even when Jupiter transits in Sagittarius and Capricorn, it will bring him good results.

4. The Aspects

As already indicated, aspects have a great influence on natives' lives if they belong to good planets. Even Saturn's aspects on its friendly signs or houses are mostly good. Jupiter sitting in the third house in the native's chart has excellent aspects on the seventh and eleventh houses. It also has a direct aspect on the ninth house which, though not a friendly sign for Jupiter, may help him to some extent when Jupiter transits the third house (in Scorpio).

Similarly, Saturn's aspects on the sixth, tenth and first houses of the native have good and bad effects. Its aspect on the seventh will make him victorious against his enemies, its aspect on the Moon will keep him worried even in small matters, and its aspect on the ascendant will make him see things from a critical angle but it also affects the relationship with his father. The native has Jupiter's positive placement in the chart. Sitting in the third house Jupiter will always help him keep good company and will be beneficial in his matrimonial life, reducing the ill effects of Ketu placed in the seventh house. He will have friends in high places. Thus, exalted Mercury and a strong Jupiter have provided much benefits and balanced the losses incurred on account of a weak Venus, Ketu and the Sun. Mercury and Jupiter will both drag him out of his current problems, which began around seven years ago. They will largely restore his status when he is 51 years old.

When the ascendant is in the exalted sign and sitting in the first house, it is bound to rescue the native from odds in his/her life. Besides, Jupiter's aspect on its own house (signs) will boost the native's luck relating to that house.

Case Study Nine

We present here the chart (*kundali*) of a female who was almost blind at birth and remained quite inactive due to her inability to see properly. However, she got a fairly good education, as her family background was quite good. She was born in southern Rajasthan and when she met us, she had played much of her early innings in life. She was almost 37 when her chart was being analysed. Her marriage is predicted around 21 years of age, but it would not have stayed for long as both Mars and Saturn have their aspects on the seventh house, which is the house predicting matters of the spouse. The chart of the native is reproduced below for further analysis.

Chart of Native Born on 15 Feb. 1967

```
                9              Ketu, Mars
                                   7
  10                  8                    6

      Sun, Mercury,
         Venus                      5
          11
  Saturn                                Jupiter
    12              2                      4
         Moon, Rahu
            1                   3
```

1. Strength of Ascendant

Mars the owner of the ascendant is sitting in the twelfth, which is the house of waste, travel, expenses and *moksha*. It is conjunct with Ketu, providing the native with some kind of artistic qualities. Besides, Mars also controls the sixth house in this chart. Thus, the ascendant, which is sitting in the twelfth, is also the owner of the house of sickness, affecting the native's health, especially the right eye. In view of all this, the ascendant is not strong enough to provide beneficial results. If it were not Jupiter's aspect on the ascendant, the native would not have cared for any kind of moral precepts in life. She does not abide by morals too much even though Jupiter has its aspect on the ascendant. We will discuss Jupiter's good effects later, when discussing aspects of the planets.

2. Fifth, Ninth and Tenth Houses

As the owner of the fifth is sitting in the ninth (luck) house, it has given her good education. She is a post-graduate in arts, probably in English Literature (on account of Saturn's placement in the fifth). Besides, the owner of the fifth is directly looking at the fifth from the ninth house. It has helped her to have some sort of continuity with education. Except that Saturn is sitting in the fifth and has reduced the good effects of that house to some extent, the fifth house of the native is quite strong. Saturn's placement has some kind of impediment towards children and reflective thinking. The owner of the tenth, Sun, is sitting in the fourth conjunct with Venus and Mercury, which also tends to draw the native's interests towards educational projects or jobs.

As the Sun (owner of the tenth) is sitting in the fourth, the native's father has to do with her habitation. Since the owner of the tenth is looking at the tenth and is conjunct with the owner of the eleventh (Mercury) and the owner of seventh (Venus), she will have considerable good benefits from her father and some benefits from her husband too for some time. She is bound to continue her efforts in educational (Mercury conjunct with the Sun) and musical (Venus conjunct with the Sun) areas. She will not sit idle and will constantly be busy with work in the fields indicated above, although her eyesight is impaired. Since the owner of the ninth (Moon) is sitting in the sixth house with Rahu, it has reduced the good effects of the ninth house, except that Jupiter sitting in the ninth house has restored its good effects to a considerable extent.

3. Seventh House

It is quite unfortunate that her married life was very short, as both Saturn and Mars are looking at the seventh house. An early disruption in the married life is also indicated by Venus conjunct

166

with a strong Sun, which eclipses it by its power, strength and warmth. Even if he had lived longer, they were bound to be separated on account of Saturn's aspect on the seventh house. But she is bound to have a number of male friends, as Jupiter is looking at the third house (house of friends) and the fifth house (amours illicit) while Saturn is sitting there.

Saturn itself is indicative of friendship and relationships as it occupies the fifth house, which is also the house of romance. Please refer to the second chapter to learn more about the benefits and other aspects of the houses.

4. The Aspects

Before concluding our analysis on the chart, we would like to briefly discuss matters relating to various aspects of the planets on different houses. Jupiter has provided much strength to the native's entire chart, as its aspects on the ascendant, third and the fifth houses restore luck relating to those houses.

Besides, it has also cured much of her physical infirmity, even relating to her eyesight, and provides her physical strength, determination and doggedness. Similarly, the Sun's aspects on the tenth house have benefited the native in terms of gains from her father and in finding errands and projects to run her life well. But Saturn's aspects on the seventh, eleventh and second have bad, good and bad effects respectively.

When Jupiter is in its exalted sign in the ninth house and looks at the ascendant, third and fifth houses, it is bound to bring longevity, good health, love for education, and strong determination. Besides, it restores the ill effects of a weak ascendant.

Case Study Ten

The following chart belongs to a celebrated Indian sportsman who became world famous at the early age of 18. Born with an exalted Sun sign and possessing an exalted Mars, he has enjoyed great reputation and admiration as a sportsman who has transcended national boundaries, earning a lot of wealth through his extraordinary display on the field. He was born in Bombay, around 31 years ago, at the time this analysis was made. His chart is given herewith for further analysis.

Renowned Sportsman Born on 24 April 1973

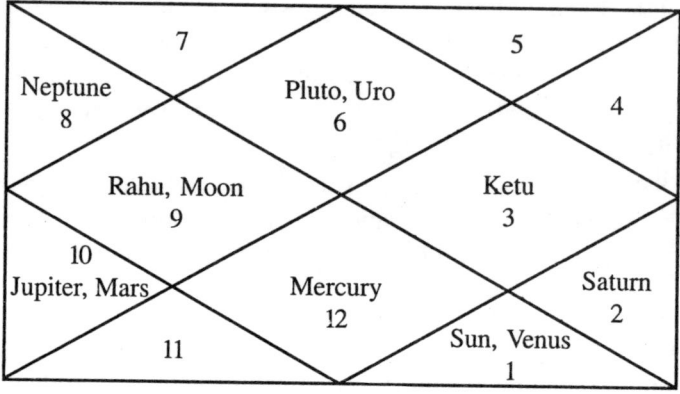

1. Strength of Ascendant

The owner of the ascendant Mercury, though debilitated, is sitting in the seventh house and is looking at the first house. As such, Mercury has its exalted aspect on its own sign, which rises in the ascendant. It is a kind of *Neechbhagna Yoga,* which simply means that although the *yogkarak* (productive and beneficial) planet is in debilitation sign, it is going to benefit the native by its look or placement, or both. Mercury looking at the ascendant with an exalted look (aspect) can make a native possess a remarkable personality. The said sportsman not only possesses a distinguished personality but has also become a national hero. Youngsters often copy him in their conduct and refer to him in discussions. How gratifying it could be for any human being to be so popular and famous, not only within his own country but throughout the world! Thus, the ascendant is very strong in the chart of the native.

2. Fifth and Ninth Houses

When we examine the fifth and ninth houses, we find that both the houses possess extraordinary strength as Mars, the owner of sports, is sitting in its exalted sign. Saturn the owner of the fifth is sitting in the ninth house, which is the house of luck. Though the owner of the ninth is rising in the eighth, it is conjunct with the exalted Sun, causing it to be blurred as well as granting it strength. Since the owner of the ninth is sitting in the twelfth house from the ninth, at times it drains the native's luck, which is again restored by Saturn (owner of fifth production) sitting in a friendly sign. Though

Jupiter is in its debilitated sign, it is conjunct with the exalted Mars, which is its permanent friend. It provides him an intelligent outlook about life and matters related to his profession. Thus, both houses have become very strong.

3. Eighth House

Though it is the house relating to death, it is also connected with hidden gains, and strength. It has become stronger by the placement of the exalted Sun, which has a direct aspect by Mars, the owner of the eighth. So, when we examine the eighth very carefully, we find that the house has some extra strength, which has been supporting the native to excel in life. There is also *Vipreet Raj Yoga*, as the owner of the twelfth is sitting in the eighth house. It not only provides fame, money and occasional travel, but also a kind of confidence hardly found in most natives.

4. The Aspects

This chart contains rather beneficial aspects on its various houses, providing the native with extraordinary luck, fortune and fame. An exalted Mars has its aspect on an exalted Sun, providing him great fame, religious and moral disposition as well as immense confidence. Besides, debilitated Jupiter's aspects on the ninth (and Saturn), eleventh (its exalted look), and the ascendant has provided the native with great luck, extraordinary financial benefits and a comely figure, adored by thousands of people throughout the world. Although the Moon is in its debilitated sign, it has an exalted look at the ninth house, which provides great opportunities, fame, luck, money and wealth.

Yet, there is another great aspect from Mercury on the native's ascendant. Sitting in the seventh house, though Mercury is also in its debilitated sign, it has its exalted aspect on its own house, which is the ascendant. It makes the native polite, decent, soft spoken, and prudent, with a handsome countenance. Like Mercury, the native is also light-footed and displays feats by his excellent game and winning style.

Case Study Eleven

We present here the chart of Sri Ramakrishna Paramhansa, who was known as God-incarnate in nineteenth century Bengal. He is one of the most respected, adored and loved human beings, not only in Bengal but all over India.

Chart of Sri Ramakrishna Born on 17 Feb. 1836

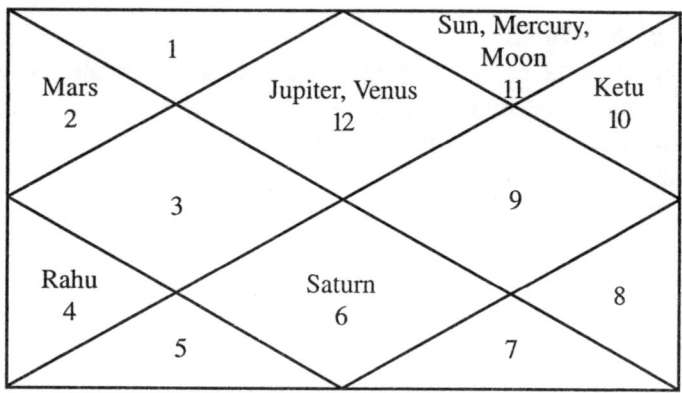

1. Strength of Ascendant

It is so obvious that the ascendant in Sri Ramakrishna's chart is extremely strong as its owner, Jupiter along with the exalted Venus, is sitting there. Jupiter being the owner of the tenth and the ascendant is in control of both houses. We reckon there is a kind of similarity in the charts of Swami Ram Tirth (case study seven) and Sri Ramakrishna. In Swami Ram Tirth's case, the ascendant Jupiter is sitting in the seventh house in Virgo along with the debilitated Venus. They both look at the *lagna*. Thus, Jupiter looks at the ascendant being its owner, while Venus has its exalted aspect on it. In Sri Ramakrishna's chart, the ascendant Jupiter is sitting in the *lagna* along with the exalted Venus. So both possessed highly beneficial aspects on their *lagna*.

Swamiji's early life, however, was quite disturbed as debilitated Venus was sitting in the seventh house, but Ramakrishna lived a devotee's life from the beginning. He participated in religious activities from an early age and started worshipping Kali at the temple of Dakshineshwar, near Calcutta. With this, we would like to draw the attention of the reader to the fact that a conjunct of Jupiter and Venus can bring tremendous effects on the native. The reader can draw inferences from both charts. Sri Ramakrishna was never attracted towards women and other worldly things but, for a considerable amount of time, Swamiji kept unhealthy company.

It shows that Venus in debilitated and exalted positions can bestow bad and good results respectively. But its conjunct with a strong Jupiter can bring very good results to the native. Its bad and good aspects can also bring similar results. Ultimately, Swamiji also reached the pinnacle in life and attained God's domain because of Venus's exalted aspect on his ascendant and Jupiter's aspect on its own house.

2. Fourth, Ninth and Tenth Houses

Though Rahu is sitting in the fourth house, it has an exalted look from Jupiter. Jupiter also looks at the ninth house, and Mars the owner of the ninth, also looks at the ninth house, which is its own house. It increases the power of the ninth house and makes Sri Ramakrishna very lucky in matters relating to God. In fact, the ninth house is the house of luck and *dharma* too. Therefore, Sri Ramakrishna never abandoned God's path in his life. Even after marriage he treated his wife as his friend. It is reported that he never ever had any physical relations with her. Jupiter is also the owner of the tenth. As a result, his father loved him dearly, and by profession he became a priest in a temple and continued that work until the end.

3. The Aspects

The aspects of Jupiter and Mars are highly beneficial and provide Sri Ramakrishna with an enlightened thought process from an early age. How he kept the company of *sadhus* when he was still in school and performed *puja* (worship) and prayers at the temple at Dakshineshwar later are noteworthy. It was his great luck (ninth house being very strong) that he met Brahmani and Totapuri as teachers one after the other. They gradually directed him to the path of devotion and helped him to finally attain godliness. The Moon, which owns the fifth house, is sitting in the twelfth house. It did not allow him to get much education. Rahu, sitting in the fifth, also disrupted his educational career.

At times he also behaved like a mentally disturbed person, crying and singing in praise of God for hours. Some writers have reported a great emotional disturbance and imbalance in Sri Ramakrishna's life. This may have happened due to the presence of Rahu in the fifth and the Moon sitting in the twelfth. But the disruption and emotional disturbance could not hamper his godly pursuits. He always followed God, as his ascendant was equipped with two great planets, Jupiter and Venus. Saturn the owner of the twelfth is sitting in the seventh and has its look at the ninth house. The twelfth being responsible for *moksha*, became helpful to him as it looks at the ninth house of the native. Thus, he was bound to grow as a highly religious person who would ultimately attain God's house.

When Jupiter rises in Pisces and sits in the **lagna,** *which is its own house and an exalted Venus also conjuncts it, it is bound to lead the native to attain God's domain finally.*

Case Study Twelve

The following chart belongs to a cinema giant whose fame has broken national boundaries, but he has seen great ups and downs in his career. No other cinema actor or actress has dominated the cinema world in India for the number of years he has ruled. As an actor he is superb and matchless. As a human being he is acclaimed to be one of the nicest persons in society, always prepared to lend a helping hand. Let us discuss his chart.

Chart of Cinema Star Born on 11 Oct. 1942

```
 12              Ketu        10
 1               11          9
       Saturn                8
       2
 3              Rahu        Moon
               5            7
       Jupiter      Mars, Sun,
       4        Mercury, Venus 6
```

1. Ascendant's Strength

The ascendant Saturn is sitting in the fourth house from the *lagna*. It has its aspect on the first house. It makes the ascendant very strong, providing the native great imagination and adaptability. As an actor, he has inborn talent, which he has proved by the types of roles he has enacted very successfully. He has seen ups and downs in life, when his ascendant has transited in good and bad signs and houses respectively. But Saturn being the owner of the ascendant has the quality to help the native during his advanced years. Consequently, he has recently been honoured by world agencies with a high position.

Currently when his chart was being analysed, Saturn is transiting Gemini, which is a very beneficial sign for Saturn. It has provided him great honour during its two and a half years of stay in that sign. Thus, the strength of the ascendant can be judged from its transits in various houses and friendly, exalted or debilitated signs.

2. Second and Eleventh Houses

The owner of the second and the eleventh, Jupiter is exalted and is sitting in the sixth house, which is not considered a good house. Besides, the owner of the eleventh house is in the eighth from there, while the owner of the second (hard-earned wealth) is in the fifth house from its ownership. It also indicates ups and downs in the native's life. However, the aspects from Jupiter on the tenth and the second houses helps the native get good and lucrative jobs, allowing him to earn money and wealth through hard work.

3. Eighth House

Four planets are conjunct in the eighth house, which is quite unusual. It could lead to injury or sickness that could mar his career and endanger his life. He has also received stomach injuries once while acting for a particular scene in a movie. But Saturn, placed in a friendly sign and strong house, has helped him come out of the injury without any lasting problems. Besides, Mercury the owner of the eighth is exalted and sitting in the eighth. It has formed *Vipreet Rajyoga*, which has provided him fame, wealth and position. Furthermore, Mercury is conjunct with the owners of the fourth, fifth, ninth and the third. As the eighth house also indicates great vigour and hidden strength, it has helped the native to come out of his turmoil very successfully.

4. The Aspects

When we examine the native's chart from the point of view of aspects, we find that Saturn's aspects on the *lagna*, tenth house and Jupiter (the owner of gains and earned wealth) has helped the native earn a lot in life. Venus' exalted aspect on the second house has further strengthened his desire and capability to earn wealth with extra vigour and determination. Mars' aspect on the third house, which is its own house, has helped him work very hard and made him extremely hard working. With Ketu sitting in *lagna* and Rahu's aspect on it, it has added to the strength of the ascendant. Jupiter's aspects on the tenth and second houses have benefited the native with good assignments and wealth. As Jupiter also has its aspect on the twelfth house, the native has been travelling, which has provided him greater benefits and opportunities. So, once again it is clear that aspects have great impact on an individual's life.

When Saturn is the ascendant, in view of its transits in good and bad signs and houses, it can provide ups and downs in one's life.

Conclusion

Before concluding this chapter, we would like to remind you that the importance of the ascendant in a chart is paramount. Swami Ram Tirth and Sri Ramakrishna's charts stand as testimonies to this fact. **The natives acquired much of their characteristics and qualities from the rising sign, the sign of the Sun in which it is transiting at the time of birth and finally from the placement and position of the owner of the ascendant.**

When we put all three together, we discover how much the native will force his/her way towards progress and affluence in life, as much depends on the native's personal qualities. Rest of the houses and the planets affect job positions (10th), luck and foreign tours (9th), household affairs and relationship with the partner and others (4th & 7th), education and children (5th), total gains in life (11th), and the likelihood of attaining *moksha* (12th).

It is, therefore, imperative that you carefully examine the first three things referred to above, when making any predictions. In testimony to what we have narrated, we would like to put forth the cases of two natives whose ascendants and rising signs bestowed qualities, benefits and demerits befitting them.

The first case is of a native born on 21 December 1937 in west Rajasthan. The rising sign in his chart is Leo and the ascendant Sun is transiting Sagittarius in the fifth house. The owner of the ninth house, Mars (luck) is sitting in the seventh house and has its friendly aspect on the ascendant. The native has retired as a senior administrative officer from the Education Department of Rajasthan around five years ago, and is keeping good health. Besides, he has a respectable position in society, which has been further enhanced by his three sons. Out of the three, two sons are highly placed in the Central Government. The third son is also doing fairly well in life. As the ascendant is well placed in the fifth house, and Mars has its aspect on it from the seventh house, it has tremendous strength. It has benefited the native with not only three good sons but with excellence in education too.

Besides attaining a Masters' degrees in English Literature and Education, he has also obtained a Ph.D. in Education. The native possesses very firm determination and his actions are the outcome of his firmness, though at times that firmness turns into rigidity in disposition. Thus, a well-placed and strong ascendant has helped the native rise in life from a second grade teacher to the District Education Officer, besides other benefits.

In contrast to the above, we present another case of a native who has plenty of money and huge properties. But as far as his personal qualities are concerned, he stoops to a very low level on many occasions as his ascendant is not well placed. This native was born in June 1934 in Uttar Pradesh. The owner of his ascendant Aries is placed in Pisces in the twelfth house, the house related to waste, expenditure, travels and other negative qualities. Although Saturn, the owner of the tenth and the eleventh houses, is placed in the eleventh house, the native has mostly benefited in terms of money, but on account of the ascendant's placement in a weak house (12th), his thought process has been greatly afflicted. The debilitated aspect from Saturn on the ascendant has led to a distortion of the native's thought process, making him indulge in fraudulent activities, generally relating to money and women. Consequently, his decisions and activities are often profit-oriented, leading him to anti-social activities and illegal dealings, resulting in a bad reputation.

Therefore, one must bear in mind that if the owner of the first house (ascendant), or the owners of the 4th, 5th, 7th, 9th or 10th

175

houses are placed in the 6th or 12th house, they become weak. As a result, they will never bestow any beneficial results on the native. Similarly, if the ascendant is sitting in the 6th or 8th house, the power of the ascendant is weakened. At this juncture, we recall the case of a native in whose chart Leo is rising. The owner of Leo, the Sun, is placed in the 6th house and the owner of the 6th house is placed in the 1st house. It simply indicates some kind of sickness. The native who is hardly 21 years of age is sick because of heavy drinking. As a result, his entire career is at stake.

We would like to mention very briefly another yoga known as *Kalsarpa Yoga*. It is formed when all the remaining planets are placed in between Rahu and Ketu. For example, if Rahu is placed in the 6th and Ketu in the 12th house, and all the other planets are between the 1st and 5th houses, *Kalsarpa Yoga* is formed. Traditionally, this is a bad yoga and does not allow the native to enjoy benefits from the other beneficial planets placed in the chart. But our experience reveals that this yoga cannot harm the native if any of the other planets are placed either with Rahu or Ketu. Besides, a strong and beneficial aspect from a beneficial ascendant can reduce the ill effects of this yoga to a considerable extent.

There is yet another yoga known as *Kemdrum Yoga*. It is formed when there is no planet on either side of the Moon. It makes the native a spendthrift. Money flows from his hands very easily, leaving him financially weak even if his earnings are great. Much cannot be done to arrest the ill effects of this yoga, except that a good pearl in a silver or gold ring should be worn by the native who has this yoga.

Before we close our discussions on the subject, we would like to draw your attention to the material highlighted in *bold italics* (each case study has a few lines highlighted) placed in between each case study. All the canons of astrology cannot be summarised in eleven precepts only that have been highlighted at the end of each case study. They can guide you and help you predict quite correctly some important matters relating to a chart and benefit the native desirous of knowing something about himself/herself. We have also specifically indicated very important Rajyogas in this chapter for the benefit of the reader. It will surely enhance the reader's perception and thought process relating to the predictive side of astrology.

References

1. Athena Starwoman, (2000), Zodiac Athena's Sun Signs: USA, Barnes & Noble.

2. Dane Rudhyar, (1972), The Astrological Houses: The Spectrum of Individual Experience; New York: Doubleday.

3. Edwin C. Krupp, (1991), Beyond the Blue Horizon; New York: HarperCollins.

4. Gary Goldschneider & Joost Elffers, (1994), The Secret Language of Birthdays: New York, Viking Penguin Books.

5. Jai Ram Mishra, (1959), Swami Ramtirth Jeevan; Allahabad: Lok Bharti Prakashan.

6. James R. Lewis, (1994), Astrology Encyclopaedia: London, Gale Research Inc.

7. Jan Spillen, (2001), New Moon Astrology: New York, Bantam Books.

8. Julia & Derek Parker, (1991), Parker's Astrology: London, A D K Publishing Books.

9. Jim Tester, (1987), A History of Western Astrology, New York: Ballantine.

10. Julia Parker, (1995), The Astrology's Handbook: Sebastopol, CA, CRCS.

11. K.M. Brielmain (Ed.) (2003), Llewellyn's @004 Sun Signs Book: St. Paul, M.N. Llewellyn Publications.

12. Kim Rogers-Gallagher, (1998), Astrology for the Light Side of the Future: Santiago CA, ACS Publications.

13. Larry Kettelkamp, (1973) Astrology - Wisdom of the Stars: New York, William Morrow Junior Books.

14. Mary Ellen Snodgrass, (1997), Signs of the Zodiac: London, Green Wood Press.

15. Madeline Gerwick-Brodeur & Lisa Lenard, (2003), Astrology, New York: Alpha.

16. Neil Somerville, (2003), Your Chine Horoscope 2004: London, Element.
17. Nicholas Campion & Steve Eddy, (1999), The New Astrology; Vermont: Trafalgar Square Publishing.
18. Nicholas Campion, (1987), The Practical Astrology; New York: Harry N. Abrams (Mercury Disruption).
19. Ralph Williams Holden, (1977), The Elements of House Divisions; Essex, U.K.: L.N. Fowler.
20. Robin Mac Naughton (1978), Sun Sign Personality Guide: New York, Bantam Books.
21. Sandra Maie, (1981), Fun Astrology: New York, Julian Messner.
22. Suzanne White, (1986), The New Astrology: New York, St. Martin's Press.

Indian Publications

23. Subramaniam K. (1994), Astrology For Beginners, Chennai: Jothi Offset, V.M. Street, Royapettah.
24. Suresh Chandra Mishra, (1996), Brihat Parasara Hora Sastram, New Delhi: Ranjan Publications, Ansari Road.
25. Pt. Krishna Ashant, (2001), Lagna Darshan Part One; Delhi: Shila Lekh Publications.
26. Pt. Krishna Ashant, (2001), Lagna Darshan, Part Two; Delhi: Shila Lekh.
27. Pt. Krishna Ashant, (2001). Lagna Darshna, Part Three; Delhi: Shila Lekh.
28. Pt. Krishna Ashant, (2001), Lagna Darshna, Part Four; Delhi: Shila Lekh.
29. Sri Mantreswar, (1969), Phal Dipika, Varanashi: Motilal Banarasidas (translated & edited by Gopesh Kumar Ojha.)
30. Major S.G. Khot, (1976), Laghu Parashari Siddhant, Varanashi: Motilal Banarasidas Pvt. Ltd.
31. Ramesh Upadhya, (2000), Jyotish Tatva, Vivek, Datia: Shree Peetamber Peeth.
32. B. Bala, (1980), Mahabala's Advance Ephemeris, Chennai: Krishnamurti Publications.
33. Concise Narad-Vishnupurannank; Special Issue on the 28th Year, Gorakhpur: Gitapress, Kalyan.

Appendices

Appendix I

Please consult any Hindi *Panchang* (calendar) to find out the exact rising sign at the time of a child's birth or to determine a chart (*kundali*). Any *Panchang* (calendar) published from Jodhpur or Jaipur (Rajasthan) or the *Vishwa Panchang* published from Benaras (Uttar Pradesh) will be good for this purpose. In each *Panchang*, the last few pages are devoted to ascertaining the rising sign (*rashi*). At the bottom of each page, 12 months' rising signs on each day (date) are listed denoting month, date, rising sign (*rashi*) and the duration of that *rashi* on a particular day.

Thus, all the 12 *rashis*, as they run on a particular day and in a particular month, run one after the other. It is just a simple method to find out the rising sign. For more details, consult a professional if you are unable to ascertain the correct rising sign.

Appendix II

The traditional rulerships of the planets are among the basic building blocks of astrological chart interpretation. These rulerships were originally assigned by astronomers/astrologers of the ancient world. However, since the 1700s astrologers have had to come to terms with the more recently discovered planets of the solar system, and to integrate them into the existing system, assigning rulers to them on a number of grounds, including world events that were occurring at the time when each planet was discovered.

Planetary Traditions

The chart on the opposite page shows when planets rule, and other traditional relationships they have with the signs.

Personal planets

The personal planets are as follows: the Sun; the Moon; the planet that is ruling the Ascendant sign (the chart ruler); the planet that is ruling the Sun sign (the Sun ruler); and the planet that is ruling the sign occupied by the Moon (the Moon ruler).

Traditional relationships

Each planet rules one or two signs of the Zodiac. These rulerships were decreed way back in the distant past. Each planet is exalted in a particular sign, from which it works well, and with the characteristics of which it has a sympathetic rapport. When a planet is placed in its sign of exaltation, its importance in an interpretation is marginally increased.

Each planet has a sign of detriment. This is the sign of the Zodiac opposite the one it rules (its polar sign). Traditional astrology decrees that the planet works less well from this sign. Each planet has a fall sign. This is the sign directly across the Zodiac (against the polar sign) from that in which it is exalted. Here, again, the planet was once thought to work less well. As with the signs of detriment, this is a factor to be kept in mind when interpreting a chart.

The modern planets

Since the discovery of the modern planets – Uranus in 1781, Neptune in 1846 and Pluto in 1930 – there has been much discussion concerning the attribution of their rulerships, and the signs in which they may be exalted or in fall.

The signs of rulership, and therefore detriment, have, apart from the planet Pluto and Chiron (discovered in 1977), have long since been debated and finalised. As will be seen from the chart:

1. Uranus rules Aquarius, so the sign of its detriment is Leo.

2. Neptune rules Pisces, so the sign of its detriment is Virgo.

3. Pluto rules Scorpio, so the sign of its detriment is Taurus.

4. There is more difficulty in determining the signs of exaltation. Many astrologers feel that Uranus is exalted in Scorpio, and Neptune is exalted in Leo.

THE GLYPHS OF THE SIGNS AND WHAT THEY REPRESENT

Sign	Glyph	What it Represents	Planet	Glyph	Rulership
Aries	♈	The Ram's Head	Sun	☉	♌ Leo
Taurus	♉	The Bull's Head	Moon	☽	♋ Cancer
Gemini	♊	The Twins	Mercury	☿	♊♍ Gemini, Virgo
Cancer	♋	Breasts	Venus	♀	♉♎ Taurus, Libra
Leo	♌	The Lion's Tail	Mars	♂	♈ Aries
Virgo	♍	Female Genitals	Jupiter	♃	♐ Sagittarius
Libra	♎	A Pair of Scales	Saturn	♄	♑ Capricorn
Scorpio	♏	Male Genitals	Uranus	♅	♒ Aquarius
Sagittarius	♐	The Centaur's Arrow	Neptune	♆	♓ Pisces
Capricorn	♑	The Goat's Head and Fish's Tail	Pluto	♇ ⯓*	♏ Scorpio
Aquarius	♒	Water, Air Waves – the Ether	Chiron	⚷	Perhaps Virgo
Pisces	♓	Two Fish			

* *The alternative glyph for Pluto is sometimes used*

Mutual Reception

Mutual reception occurs when Planet A is in a sign that is ruled by Planet B, and Planet B is in a sign that is ruled by Planet A. So, the Moon may be in Scorpio and Pluto in Cancer, or as here – Mercury in Sagittarius and Jupiter in Gemini or Virgo. The planets involved are in harmony and, if

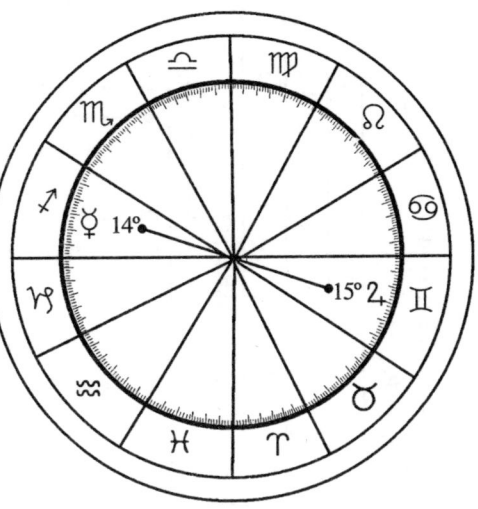

they also make aspect to each other, the strength of that aspect is slightly increased. Should the aspect be a square, opposition or minor negative aspect, any tension indicated will be mitigated, since the planets will strengthen the psychological integration of the subject. If both are personal planets, the relationship between them will be more important.

The Strengths of the Planets				
Planet	**Rules**	**Exalted**	**Detriment**	**Fall**
Sun	♌	♈	♒	♎
Moon	♋	♉	♑	♏
Mercury	♊♍	♍	♐	♓
Venus	♉♎	♓	♈	♍
Mars	♈♏	♑	♎	♋
Jupiter	♐♓	♋	♊	♑
Saturn	♑♒	♎	♋	♈
Uranus	♒	♏	♌	♉
Neptune	♓	♌	♍	♒
Pluto	♏	♍	♉	♓

185

Appendix III

Duration of Dasa, Bhukti and Anthra in Vimshottari Dasa (120-year life period)

Dasa = Major Period; Bhukti = Sub Period; Anthra = Inter Period

IX. Mercury : 17 Years (Ashlesha or Ayilyam, Jyeshta or Kettai, Revathi nakshatras)

Anthras (in order)	1. Mercury M D	2. Kethu M D	3. Venus M D	4. Sun M D	5. Moon M D	6. Mars M D	7. Rahu M D	8. Jupiter M D	9. Saturn M D
1. Mercury	4 3	1 20	4 25	1 14	2 13	1 21	4 10	3 26	4 17
2. Kethu	1 20	0 20	1 29	0 18	1 0	0 21	1 24	1 17	1 27
3. Venus	4 25	2 0	5 20	1 21	2 25	1 29	5 3	4 16	5 12
4. Sun	1 13	0 18	1 21	0 15	0 25	0 18	1 16	1 11	1 18
5. Moon	2 12	1 0	2 25	0 26	1 12	1 0	2 17	2 8	2 20
6. Mars	1 21	0 20	2 0	0 18	1 0	0 21	1 23	1 18	1 27
7. Rahu	4 10	1 24	5 3	1 15	2 16	1 23	4 18	4 2	4 25
8. Jupiter	3 26	1 18	4 16	1 11	2 8	1 18	4 2	3 19	4 10
9. Saturn	4 17	1 27	5 11	1 18	2 21	1 26	4 25	4 9	5 3
Total:	2-4-27	0-11-27	2-10-00	0-10-06	1-5-00	0-11-27	2-6-18	2-3-06	2-8-09

(Column group header: BHUKTIES IN EVERY DASA)

Note: In Vimshottari Dasa system of directing, the normal span of life of a human is assumed to be 120 years, which is unevenly distributed among the nine significators in a certain cyclic order. Each DASA (major period), is divided into nine Bhukties (sub periods) in the same cyclic order and proportion. Bhukties are similarly divided, unevenly, into Anthras (inter periods). Further division of Anthras yields Sookshama (sub-inter periods) and of Sookshama periods Pranas (prana dasa).

Cumulative Periods in Vimshottari Dasa

	BHUKTIES								
	1	2	3	4	5	6	7	8	9
	Y M D	Y M D	Y M D	Y M D	Y M D	Y M D	Y M D	Y M D	Y M D

(1) KETHU MAHADASA (7 years of 120 years)
Aswini (1), Makha (10) and Moola (19)

Anthras (in order)	Kethu Y M D	Sukra (Venus) Y M D	Surya (Sun) Y M D	Chandra (Moon) Y M D	Mangal (Mars) Y M D	Rahu Y M D	Guru (Jupiter) Y M D	Sani (Saturn) Y M D	Budha (Mercury) Y M D
Kethu	0 0 9	1 6 27	1 10 12	2 4 17	2 9 16	3 7 3	4 5 3	5 3 17	6 2 14
Sukra	0 1 3	0 7 7	1 11 3	2 5 22	2 10 10	3 9 6	4 6 29	5 5 23	6 4 14
Surya	0 1 10	0 7 28	1 7 3	2 6 3	2 10 18	3 9 24	4 7 16	5 6 13	6 5 2
Chandra	0 1 23	0 9 3	1 7 14	1 11 20	2 11 0	3 10 26	4 8 14	5 7 17	6 6 1
Mangal	0 2 1	0 9 27	1 7 21	2 0 3	2 6 12	3 11 18	4 9 4	5 8 10	6 6 22
Rahu	0 2 23	1 0 0	1 8 10	2 1 4	2 7 4	3 0 27	4 10 24	5 10 10	6 8 16
Guru	0 3 13	1 1 26	1 8 27	2 2 2	2 7 23	3 2 17	4 1 3	6 0 3	6 10 3
Sani	0 4 6	1 4 3	1 9 17	2 3 5	2 8 16	3 4 17	4 2 26	5 0 27	7 0 0
Budha	0 4 27	1 6 2	1 10 5	2 14 5	2 9 7	3 6 10	4 4 14	5 2 24	6 1 24

Cumulative Periods in Vimshottari Dasa

BHUKTIES								
1	2	3	4	5	6	7	8	9
Y M D	Y M D	Y M D	Y M D	Y M D	Y M D	Y M D	Y M D	Y M D

(2) SUKRA MAHADASA (20 years of 120 years)
Barani (2), P. Phalguni (11) and P. Ashada (20)

Anthras (in order)	Sukra (Venus)	Surya (Sun)	Chandra (Moon)	Mangal (Mars)	Rahu	Guru (Jupiter)	Sani (Saturn)	Budha (Mercury)	Kethu
Sukra	0 6 20	4 4 0	5 11 0	7 0 4	9 7 3	11 11 2	14 5 28	17 0 14	19 1 4
Surya	0 8 20	3 4 18	6 0 0	7 0 25	9 8 27	12 0 20	14 7 25	17 2 5	19 1 25
Chandra	1 0 0	3 5 18	4 5 20	7 2 0	9 11 27	12 3 10	14 11 0	17 5 0	19 3 0
Mangal	1 2 10	3 6 9	4 6 25	6 0 24	10 2 0	12 5 5	15 1 7	17 6 29	19 3 25
Rahu	1 8 10	3 8 3	4 9 25	6 2 47	7 7 12	12 10 0	15 6 28	18 0 12	19 5 28
Guru	2 1 20	3 9 21	5 0 15	6 4 23	8 0 6	10 6 8	16 0 0	18 4 18	19 7 24
Sani	2 8 0	3 11 18	5 3 20	6 7 0	8 5 27	10 11 10	13 4 0	18 10 0	19 10 0
Budha	3 1 20	4 1 9	5 6 15	6 8 29	8 11 0	11 3 26	13 9 12	16 4 24	20 0 0
Kethu	3 4 0	4 2 0	5 7 20	6 9 24	9 1 3	11 5 22	13 11 18	16 6 24	18 10 24

(3) SURYA MAHADASA (6 years of 120 years)

Kartik (3), U. Phalguni (12) and U. Ashada (21)

Anthras (in order)	Surya (Sun)			Chandra (Moon)			Mangal (Mars)			Rahu			Guru (Jupiter)			Sani (Saturn)			Budha (Mercury)			Kethu			Sukra (Venus)		
Surya	0	0	5	0	9	18	1	1	13	1	11	2	2	7	12	3	4	23	4	1	25	4	8	29	5	2	18
Chandra	0	0	14	0	4	3	1	1	24	1	11	29	2	8	6	3	5	21	4	2	21	4	9	9	5	3	18
Mangal	0	0	21	0	4	13	0	9	25	2	0	18	2	8	23	3	6	11	4	3	9	4	9	16	5	4	9
Rahu	0	1	7	0	5	10	0	10	14	1	3	13	2	10	6	3	8	2	4	4	25	4	10	5	5	6	3
Guru	0	1	21	0	6	4	0	11	1	1	4	26	2	1	26	3	9	18	4	6	6	4	10	22	5	7	21
Sani	0	2	8	0	7	3	0	11	21	1	6	17	2	3	12	3	0	0	4	7	24	4	11	12	5	9	18
Budha	0	2	24	0	7	8	1	0	9	1	8	3	2	4	23	3	1	19	3	11	1	5	0	0	5	11	9
Kethu	0	3	0	0	8	9	1	0	16	1	8	22	2	5	10	3	2	8	3	11	19	4	8	1	6	0	0
Sukra	0	3	18	0	9	9	1	1	7	1	10	16	2	6	28	3	4	5	4	1	10	4	8	22	5	2	0

Cumulative Periods in Vimshottari Dasa

	BHUKTIES								
	1	2	3	4	5	6	7	8	9
	Y M D	Y M D	Y M D	Y M D	Y M D	Y M D	Y M D	Y M D	Y M D

(4) CHANDRA MAHADASA (10 years of 120 years)

Rohini (4), Hastha (13) and Sravana (22)

Anthras (in order)	Chandra (Moon)	Mangal (Mars)	Rahu	Guru (Jupiter)	Sani (Saturn)	Budha (Mercury)	Kethu	Sukra (Venus)	Surya (Sun)
Chandra	0 0 25	1 5 0	2 9 28	3 11 20	5 3 15	6 6 15	7 5 15	8 4 0	9 6 24
Mangal	0 1 12	0 10 12	2 11 0	4 0 18	5 4 18	6 7 15	7 5 27	8 5 5	9 7 4
Rahu	0 2 27	0 11 14	1 7 21	4 3 0	5 7 14	6 10 1	7 6 29	8 8 5	9 8 1
Guru	0 4 7	1 0 12	1 10 3	3 1 4	5 10 0	7 0 9	7 7 27	8 10 25	9 8 25
Sani	0 5 25	1 1 15	2 0 28	3 3 20	4 6 0	7 3 0	7 9 0	9 2 0	9 9 24
Budha	0 7 7	1 2 15	2 3 15	3 5 28	4 8 21	6 0 12	7 10 0	9 4 25	9 10 19
Kethu	0 7 25	1 2 27	2 4 16	3 6 26	4 9 24	6 1 12	7 3 12	9 6 0	9 11 0
Sukra	0 9 15	1 4 2	2 7 16	3 9 16	5 0 29	6 4 7	7 4 17	8 1 10	10 0 0
Surya	0 10 0	1 4 12	2 8 13	3 10 10	5 1 28	6 5 2	7 4 28	8 2 10	9 6 9

(5) MANGAL (SEVVAI) MAHADASA (7 years of 120 years)

Mrigasira (5), Chitra (14) and Dhanishta (23)

Anthras (in order)	Mangal (Mars)			Rahu			Guru (Jupiter)			Sani (Saturn)			Budha (Mercury)			Kethu			Sukra (Venus)			Surya (Sun)			Chandra (Moon)		
Mangal	0	0	9	1	5	15	2	3	1	3	2	7	4	0	19	4	7	28	5	3	24	6	1	18	6	6	0
Rahu	0	1	1	0	6	24	2	4	21	3	4	7	4	2	13	4	8	20	5	5	27	6	2	7	6	7	1
Guru	0	1	20	0	8	14	1	7	0	3	6	0	4	4	0	4	9	10	5	7	23	6	2	24	6	7	29
Sani	0	2	13	0	10	14	1	8	23	2	6	24	4	5	27	4	10	3	5	10	0	6	3	14	6	9	2
Budha	0	3	4	1	0	7	1	10	11	2	8	21	3	7	21	4	10	24	5	11	29	6	4	2	6	10	2
Kethu	0	3	13	1	1	0	1	11	0	2	9	14	3	8	11	4	6	6	6	0	24	6	4	9	6	10	14
Sukra	0	4	7	1	3	3	2	0	26	2	11	20	3	10	11	4	7	0	5	1	4	6	5	0	6	11	11
Surya	0	4	15	1	3	21	2	1	13	3	0	10	3	10	29	4	7	7	5	1	25	6	1	0	7	0	0
Chandra	0	4	27	1	4	23	2	2	11	3	1	14	3	11	28	4	7	20	5	3	0	6	1	11	6	5	17

Cumulative Periods in Vimshottari Dasa

	BHUKTIES								
	1	2	3	4	5	6	7	8	9
	Y M D	Y M D	Y M D	Y M D	Y M D	Y M D	Y M D	Y M D	Y M D

(6) RAHU MAHADASA (18 years of 120 years)
Arudhra (6), Swathi (15) and Sathabisha (24)

Anthras (in order)	Rahu			Guru (Jupiter)			Sani (Saturn)			Budha (Mercury)			Kethu			Sukra (Venus)			Surya (Sun)			Chandra (Moon)			Mangal (Mars)		
Rahu	0	4	26	5	1	6	7	6	25	9	9	2	11	1	4	13	0	27	14	10	9	15	10	19	17	2	11
Guru	0	9	5	3	0	7	7	11	12	10	1	5	11	2	25	13	5	21	14	11	22	16	1	1	17	3	21
Sani	1	2	9	3	4	24	5	6	18	10	6	0	11	4	24	13	11	12	15	1	13	16	3	27	17	5	21
Budha	1	6	27	3	8	26	5	11	14	8	3	22	11	6	18	14	4	15	15	2	29	16	6	13	17	7	15
Kethu	1	8	3	3	10	17	6	1	14	8	5	16	10	6	22	14	6	18	15	3	18	16	7	15	17	8	7
Sukra	2	2	6	4	3	11	6	7	5	8	10	19	10	8	25	12	0	18	15	5	12	16	10	15	17	10	10
Surya	2	3	24	4	4	24	6	8	26	9	0	4	10	9	14	12	2	12	14	7	4	16	11	12	17	10	28
Chandra	2	6	15	4	7	6	6	11	21	9	2	21	10	10	15	12	5	12	14	8	1	15	6	27	18	0	0
Mangal	2	8	12	4	8	26	7	1	21	9	4	15	10	11	7	12	7	15	14	8	20	15	7	28	17	0	4

(7) GURU MAHADASA (16 years of 120 years)
Punarvasu (7), Visakha (16) and P. Bhadra (25)

Anthras (in order)	Guru (Jupiter)	Sani (Saturn)	Budha (Mercury)	Kethu	Sukra (Venus)	Surya (Sun)	Chandra (Moon)	Mangal (Mars)	Rahu
Guru	0 3 12	4 8 0	6 6 27	0 7 01	9 6 28	10 10 29	11 10 24	12 11 25	14 3 11
Sani	0 7 14	2 6 12	6 11 6	7 8 24	10 0 0	11 0 14	12 1 10	13 1 18	14 7 28
Budha	0 11 3	2 10 22	4 11 26	7 10 12	10 4 16	11 1 25	12 3 18	13 3 6	15 0 0
Kethu	1 0 18	3 0 15	5 1 13	6 11 26	10 6 12	11 2 12	12 4 16	13 3 25	15 1 20
Sukra	1 4 26	3 5 17	5 5 29	7 1 22	8 3 22	11 4 0	12 7 6	13 5 21	15 6 14
Surya	1 6 4	3 7 2	5 7 10	7 2 8	8 5 10	10 6 26	12 8 0	13 6 8	15 7 28
Chandra	1 8 8	3 9 18	5 9 18	7 3 6	8 8 0	10 7 20	11 5 0	13 7 6	15 10 10
Mangal	1 9 23	3 11 12	5 11 6	7 3 26	8 9 26	10 8 7	11 6 8	12 8 20	16 0 0
Rahu	2 1 18	4 3 28	6 3 8	7 5 16	9 2 20	10 9 20	11 8 20	12 10 0	13 11 16

Cumulative Periods in Vimshottari Dasa

BHUKTIES

1	2	3	4	5	6	7	8	9
Y M D	Y M D	Y M D	Y M D	Y M D	Y M D	Y M D	Y M D	Y M D

(8) SANI MAHADASA (15 years of 120 years)
Pushya (8), Anuradha (17) and U. Bhadra (26)

Anthras (in order)	Sani (Saturn)			Budha (Mercury)			Kethu			Sukra (Venus)			Surya (Sun)			Chandra (Moon)			Mangal (Mars)			Rahu			Guru (Jupiter)		
Sani	0	5	21	5	8	12	6	7	24	9	4	3	10	6	28	11	10	5	13	0	22	14	10	15	17	2	14
Budha	0	10	25	3	4	20	7	9	21	9	9	14	10	8	16	12	0	26	13	2	19	15	3	10	17	6	23
Kethu	1	0	28	3	6	17	5	9	5	9	11	21	10	9	6	12	1	29	13	3	12	15	5	10	17	8	16
Sukra	1	6	29	3	11	28	5	11	12	7	4	1	10	11	3	12	5	4	13	5	19	15	11	1	18	1	18
Surya	1	8	23	4	1	17	6	0	2	7	5	28	10	0	8	12	6	3	13	6	9	16	0	23	18	3	4
Chandra	1	11	23	4	4	7	6	1	5	7	9	3	10	1	7	11	0	20	13	7	12	16	3	18	18	5	20
Mangal	2	1	26	4	6	4	6	1	28	7	11	9	10	1	27	11	1	24	12	6	26	16	5	18	18	7	13
Rahu	2	7	9	4	10	29	6	3	28	8	5	0	10	3	18	11	4	19	12	8	26	14	0	16	19	0	0
Guru	3	0	3	5	3	9	6	5	21	8	10	2	10	5	3	11	7	5	12	10	19	14	5	3	16	9	20

(9) BUDHA MAHADASA (17 years of 120 years)

Ashlesha (9), Jyeshta (18) and Revathi (27)

Anthras (in order)	Budha (Mercury)			Kethu			Sukra (Venus)			Surya (Sun)			Chandra (Moon)			Mangal (Mars)			Rahu			Guru (Jupiter)			Sani (Saturn)		
Budha	0	4	3	3	4	24	6	0	24	6	10	21	8	1	10	9	1	19	10	11	22	13	0	9	15	1	12
Kethu	0	5	23	2	5	18	6	2	24	6	11	9	8	2	9	9	2	10	11	1	16	13	1	26	15	3	8
Sukra	0	10	18	2	7	17	3	10	14	7	1	0	8	5	4	9	4	9	11	6	19	13	6	12	15	8	20
Surya	1	0	1	2	8	5	4	10	5	6	3	9	8	6	0	9	4	27	11	8	5	13	7	23	15	10	8
Chandra	1	2	13	2	9	5	4	3	0	6	4	5	7	2	12	9	5	27	11	10	21	13	10	1	16	0	29
Mangal	1	4	4	2	9	26	4	4	29	6	4	23	7	3	12	8	6	21	12	0	15	13	11	19	16	2	25
Rahu	1	8	14	2	11	19	4	10	2	6	6	9	7	5	29	8	8	14	9	10	15	14	3	21	16	7	21
Guru	2	0	10	3	1	7	5	2	18	6	7	19	7	8	7	8	10	2	10	2	17	12	4	4	17	0	0
Sani	2	4	27	3	3	3	5	8	0	6	9	8	7	10	27	8	11	28	10	7	12	12	8	13	14	8	24

Astrology for Layman

—Dr. T.M. Rao

The most comprehensible book to learn Astrology

Astrology today is universally recognised to be a 'science', based on sound mathematical principles and calculations. But while it is easy to agree with this promise, it is difficult to find a well-researched comprehensible book to guide the general reader. Answering this need, 'Astrology for Layman' is designed to bring home to the reader the fundamentals of the discipline along with the predictive aspect.

The book is a complete astrological guide that begins from the basic fundamentals viz. how 12 *rashis* have been formulated, the basic principles of casting a horoscope, what are the qualities ascribed to people born under different signs (for instance, people born under Aries are of independent view), what's the meaning of *Bhavas* (viz. what does a planet indicate in a specific house), what do the *Mahadashas* of different planets mean, what are 'yogas' (for instance, 'Sakaka yoga' makes a person stubborn and hated by relatives and 'Parvata yoga', makes a person passionate) – besides offering special section on the subjects of matrimony, compatibility along with case studies predicting major events of a person's life like career-change, gain or loss of fortune, etc.

Demy Size • Pages: 184
Price: Rs. 80/- • Postage: Rs. 15/-

Marriage-Matching Astrologically

—T.M. Rao

- 'Marriages are made in Heaven' — discover its true essence
- How stars influence your marriage
- Find the 'made-for-each other' partners through horoscope matching

There have been many astrological books on marriage-matching available in the market—but most of them deal only with certain aaspects and not all the essential information are available at one place.

The aim of this book is to put in a concise form all the essential principles of 'Marriage-Matching' so that the readers can have their satisfaction of getting all the information at one place. This book tells us how to dispel the unnecessary and unknown fears that may crop up in the selection of *bride* or *groom*. It also tells us how the Divine approval and blessings of heavenly stars play the role on the search for perfect combination.

❖ Know how stars influence the marriage ❖ Find the right partner through correct horoscope matching ❖ Ensure remedial measures to pacify conflicting *Nakshatras* and *Rashis* in the event of mismatch.

Demy Size • Pages: 142
Price: Rs. 80/- • Postage: Rs. 15/-

LAL KITAB
A Rare Book On Astrology

—Prof. U.C. Mahajan

English version of a very famous and rare book 'Lal Kitab', originally published in Urdu

A book on Astrology – Horoscope Reading Made Easy – was published in 2000 by Pustak Mahal, authored by Prof. U.C. Mahajan. The English version of Lal Kitab is an extension of the earlier book and both complement each other. Renowned astrologer, Roop Lal wrote Lal Kitab in Urdu, during the 19th century, based on an ancient text.

The salient points of this book are:

1. Every planet has a benefic or malefic effect according to its raashi and placement in a particular house. For example, Jupiter in house no.1 can exercise good or bad effects according to its nature, whether excellent or debilitating. Consequently, the author has classified the effect of every planet – good or bad – separately. The earlier book carried a generalised interpretation. Now, readers will find it easy to comprehend every planet's effect.

2. More case studies have been added to make it broad-based.

3. New chapters on a house, the effect of auspicious and inauspicious planets, precious stones and their significance, characteristics of all planets, nakshatras and their importance, Natal Moon chart and Saturn's transit (*Saade-Saati*) i.e., 7½ years of Saturn's malefic transit through the Moon, have been added.

4. Preparation of birth chart according to south Indian traditions has also been included.

Big Size • Pages: 336 (Hardbound)
Price: Rs. 240/- • Postage: Rs. 25/-

Horoscope Reading
Made Easy & Self-Learning

—U.C. Mahajan

Peep into your and your near
& dear one's future

Astrology by now is a tried and tested science, backed by centuries of analysis and interpretation. The planetary position in the individual charts, the causes and effects of specific conjunctions, the role of sun signs and ascendants—all the aspects of this discipline have been studied in depth by astrologers.

But for the reader, what makes the difference is the presentation of the material—and that's where this book scores over many others.

With a unique format by making extensive use of tables, point-by-point elucidation, explanatory notes and analysis, the book makes an interesting, easy and lucid readable volume. Backed by a thorough research of ancient astrology books of Urdu and English, the volume is a ready-reckoner for self-learners. What are the remedies for adverse star positions? What makes for long or short lines? How is marital bliss indicated in a particular chart? All this and whatever you're looking for is explained here in depth and detail. A must for every serious student of astrology.

Big Size • Pages: 248
Price: Rs. 135/- • Postage: Rs. 15/-

Palmistry for Beginners
—Richard Webster

Discover how the ancient science of palmistry — which has been used as an accurate tool for self-knowledge for thousands of years— can lead you to a better understanding of yourself and others.

Learn how to assess a palm at a glance, determine compatibility between couples, help people choose their ideal career – and gain a greater understanding of yourself. The book will enable complete novice to learn how to read palms as quickly as possible, but it will also serve as a valuable reference for experts. Whether you are interested in taking up palmistry professionally or just for fun, you will find this book an exceptionally easy-to-use guide to the fascinating language of the palm.

- Gain new insights into the personalities, talents and ambitions of yourself and everyone you meet
- Locate specific palm lines easily with the 181 clear, large-sized hand drawings
- Determine your friends', family's and your own future in the areas of health, money, travel, romance and children
- Learn what career you would be best at and most enjoy
- Find out what loop pattern, lines, shape of hand and length of fingers mean
- Easily discover whether two people are compatible or not

Demy Size • Pages: 282
Price: Rs. 88/- • Postage: Rs. 15/-

Explore the Power of Astrology—TRIKONA
—Dr. A.P. Parashar
Dr. V.K. Parashar

Inspired by their first book, **Explore the Power of Astrology** Dr. Ambika Prasad Parashar and his son Dr. Vinod Kumar Parashar once again offer a fresh and advanced perspective on the three important angles (houses) of the chart (kundali) traditionally known as TRIKONA, which are, the ascendant, the fifth and the ninth houses. These three houses deal with the most important areas of one's life, such as, the self, individual temperament, appearance and level of self-awareness; creativity, children and romance; religion and philosophy, extensive journeys including foreign travel, higher education, publishing and language, respectively. The book deals very extensively how these three houses influence one's life constantly and how the planets, when own these houses, influence individual's life. The authors have also analysed 36 case studies in relation to these three houses and have discussed elaborately how planets play their role in the growth of human beings.

Demy Size • Pages: 208
Price: Rs. 125/- • Postage: Rs. 15/-